VIVA

salento dwellings

Edited by Luciana Di Virgilio
Photos by Filippo Bamberghi

salento dwellings

THE MEDITERRANEAN DREAM

Foreword by **Helen Mirren**

Texts by Patrizia Piccinini
Drawings by Gianni Veneziano

New York · Paris · London · Milan

FOREWORD

Salento, the southernmost region of Apulia, stretches into the embrace of two seas, the Ionian and the Adriatic, or the Gulf of Otranto. It is a strip of land that in the first glance has little of outstanding natural beauty, apart from a lovely sea and a rocky coastline, sprinkled with caves and inviting beaches. It has no mountains, no forests, no rivers.

It hides its great charm, its intense power, behind walls and doors that hint of the beauty within, and behind winding country roads that meander across the landscape, through fields inhabited by beings out of a fairy-tale book, the monumental ancient olive trees that have commanded this landscape for centuries. Salento is the Olive and the Olive is Salento. They are now under the terrible threat of Xylella. We pray for their survival.

This is the story of Salento, the story of a rich red earth, and a beautiful pale stone that has been fashioned, over the centuries, into country walls, churches, farmers outbuildings called *pajare*, statues, magnificent cities, and *masserie*, the massive country farm houses, fortified against the many invaders to this land.

It is a story of a courageous and resilient community, who repelled those invaders, who survived great hardship and isolation, and who, now, no matter where they are in the world, are forever connected to this land. Their story is a mystery, a thriller, and a romance, and, of course, sometimes a comedy, when seen through the eyes of Checco Zalone.

Salento does not give up itself easily, but like all things earned, its riches are endless.

Helen Mirren

PREFACE

dreams are signs

Luciana Di Virgilio

Under the warm summer Salento sun, as the wind was blowing and carrying with it the scent of the sea and the land, that was the moment when everything became clear. My mind was filled with images and memories, a mosaic of places and people who spoke to me of Puglia, my native land. Yes, it was a dream, but it was also a sign: an invitation to describe and share that beauty, and to make tangible what seemed so ephemeral. Thus was born this tribute to the area known as Salento, the emotional connection to places, thoughts, people, and dreams. This project, which I curated—having worked for years with Gianni Veneziano on a path that is dedicated to the many facets of art—is meant to be much more than an interior architecture book. For me, listening and respecting the place itself is what is most essential, before any renovation project.

Every space has its history, its identity, and it is only by reaffirming its essence that we can create authentic, significant, and ethical environments. And Puglia, for me, with its timeless beauty and rich culture, is an endless source of inspiration.

The Mediterranean Dream—the subtitle I chose for my story—is a symphony of the tales of lives lived and paths followed, a plethora of Cabinets of Curiosity celebrating this borderland that has always been a cultural crossroads.

It is easy to become lost in the Neverland of François Man in Bagnolo, or to feel like a stage actor in the world of Athena McAlpine in Marittima. And again, driven by the wind, arrive in Depressa to become one's own protagonist, like in a film by Edoardo Winspeare. In Spongano you can don the clothes worn by Alina, a character in the novel *Casa Rossa* by Francesca Marciano. And you can follow Peter Benson Miller to Giuggianello, on a journey to elsewhere. You can be enchanted, as is the case of Francesco Russo, by a tower, a sign of rural pride. And then there's the return, physical as well as symbolic, suggested by Michele Sambin, a Paduan who found a home in Cannole. Lastly, you can discover Sunday lunch, on a sunny day in Nardò, seated at the table with Guy Martin.

You need to know how to recognize the signs, like on that warm day in Salento, when the wind, the sea, and the light whispered a dream in my ear. A dream that wanted to take shape, to be concrete, like a gesture that turns into a story. Thus was born La Casa dei Disegni (The House of Drawings), our home and a safe haven—for me, Gianni, and our young daughter, Virginia. A living story that grows with us, a tune that marks the days and links the tales of those who live there, a way of inhabiting and listening to space, like an embrace between dream and reality. I believe in dreams, and I also believe in the strength of those who make them come true. I believe in the Mediterranean South, in its stories, traditions, and cultures, and I believe in that purest of calls of which it is the bearer.

I am grateful to the people who live in these places and take care of them lovingly, places that are sentinels of beauty. I am grateful to those who believe in the strength of beauty, sharing and spreading it each and every day. With this book, I invite you to discover these places, their beauty, art, and life from a new, authentic perspective. Love architecture and their souls, because they always hold a profound message. And as I remember my father, to whom I dedicate this book, I feel that every word holds a small piece of his soul. Mine, ours, and everyone's.

Love is more.

SALENTO
NARDÒ
BAGNOLO DEL S.
CANNOLE
GIUGGIANELLO
SPONGANO
MARITTIMA
DE PRESSA
SALVE

CONTENTS

INTRODUCTION
With Its Heart Always Open
Patrizia Piccinini
17

1.
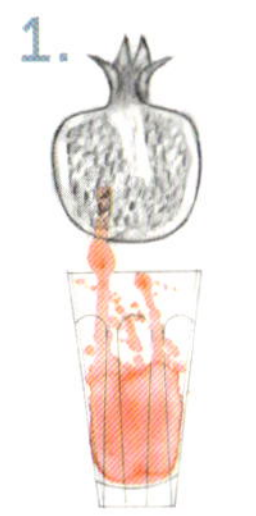
SPONGANO 22
If One Day a Female Traveler

2.

GIUGGIANELLO 42
Toward Another Place

3.

CANNOLE 74
Back to the Fold

4.
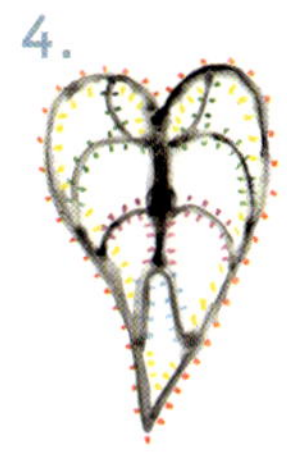
MARITTIMA 96
The Theater of the World

5.

BAGNOLO DEL SALENTO 124
Neverland

6.

SPONGANO 146
The House of Drawings

7.

NARDÒ 170
Sunday Lunch

8.

SALVE 190
The Tower's Winning Move

9.

DEPRESSA 214
By Dint of Being Wind

INTRODUCTION

with its heart always open

Patrizia Piccinini

Some roads lead to a destiny more than to a destination.
(Jules Verne)

Identifying the sense of a place means first of all abandoning oneself to the geography of the soul, a maze in which maps are of no use, where the only compass is the instinct that guides the traveler's wandering steps, spurred by an insatiable curiosity and by the deep desire to discover what dwells in the shadows of one's spirit. It is an invisible force, an occult power that lies between the currents of two seas eternally battling each other, joined solely by a quirk of fate. It is there, among the centuries-old olive trees, bent over by time and the heat, that have ceased delighting the world with the rustling of leaves destroyed by Xylella, the disease that struck the local olive trees. There, in the golden fields of wheat growing wild, blonde tresses caressed by the light wave in the wind like the sea in a storm. The red earth, scorched by the hot sun, is dotted with the green trees that have evolved to resist everything. And the houses, if not a milky white, are a hue that reminds you of honey and stone, soft and enveloping, inlaid like ancient prayers, carved in the hearts of the churches and palazzi that tell the stories of artisanal hands and eyes turned heavenward. A panorama of dwellings, the wise custodians of ancient knowledge, rising up in perfect harmony with the hot weather, offering shelter in the shaded courtyards, where the air blows gently.

Describing this part of Puglia, known as the Basso Salento (Lower Salento), isn't easy. It's not enough to offer a couple of addresses of wonderful beaches, a *masseria*[1] where guests can sleep and eat, and experience a "wow effect," or four unmissable things that can all be done in one day in Lecce. This province is not just a destination, it is an encounter that possesses all the magic of a vision, as it did for Guido Piovene, who in his *Viaggio in Italia* told his readers how Salento is actually "a land of mirages."[2] Or as Cesare Brandi wrote, in *Pellegrino di Puglia*, a "clear morning, a morning of liquid sun: and while it, the morning, may always be the same, you will never be bored by it."[3] Perhaps one needs the eye of a refined film director and intellectual like Pier Paolo Pasolini, and to imagine being on board that Fiat 1100 with him, headed on a long trip down the peninsula as far as Santa Maria di Leuca. A journey among the Italies on holiday at the dawning of the economic boom, titled "La lunga strada di sabbia" (The Long Road of Sand) and published in 1959 in the magazine *Successo*.[4] Pasolini, however, paints a memory: "Taranto is a perfect city. Living there is like living inside a shell, that of an open oyster." It was July 1959, and exactly one year later, on July 9, 1960, the first stone was laid for Italsider, the largest Italian steelworks plant. The rest is history: the birth of ILVA, the bankruptcies, the sales, and the pain of a city that over the years had to decide whether it should die of hunger or disease.

But the people of the Salento region are more resistant than any kind of metal, stronger than the blast furnaces, and they have big, calm hearts. Even when it comes to what's fashionable, this region responds with its own time, maintaining its genuine character, and today, now that it has become one of the coolest places to be, it continues to reveal its uniqueness. In Gallipoli, Porto Cesareo, Otranto, Torre dell'Orso, by now in the "least known Italian coastline"—to quote Pasolini once more—the reservations pour in, especially in August, thanks to the sea, the beauty of the terrain, and the night of San Rocco in Torrepaduli, and that of the Taranta in Melpignano. Places that have become famous for that Dionysian ritual in which musical exorcism morphs into dance. It is a bitter, ancient chant that rises up from the parched soil, a lament that becomes rhythm and then movement, like a wound that opens up to the sky and begs for mercy. It is the dance of women with furrowed faces, who in the heat of a timeless summer abandon themselves to a rite that knows no masters, where the music is nothing other than the distant echo of a pain that sinks its roots in centuries of toil and dust. In this vortex, the tambourine is the war drum but also that of festivity, the sound that shakes the earth and reawakens the drowsy spirits. And they, the *tarantolate*, wave their red handkerchiefs like the standards of an ancient pain, challenging the poison that courses through their veins, seeking salvation in a dance that is at the same time a prison and a liberation. It is the voice of the South that does not give up, it is the voice of those who have learned to thrive on very little but with dignity. It is the strength to resist, to love, and to hope again under the same sky, above the earth that welcomes the feverish steps of the *tarantolate*, and that sees the patron saints file by, transported on shoulders with the slow pace of prayers during religious feasts. Sacred and profane, as in Scorrano, a small town twenty miles from Lecce: each year on the occasion of the Feast Day of Saint Dominica, the town's patron saint is lit up with fairy lights that even Las Vegas might envy. It is thanks to an ancient miracle: salvation from the plague in exchange for a light shining in every window.

In this land, where the *Griko* dialect continues to echo in Grecìa Salentina (Salentine Greece), the discovery trip is a continuous journey back in time. It starts from far away, from the first human beings who inhabited the peninsula before the Messapians, whose traces are safeguarded in the Grotta Romanelli near Castro, the mythical site where Aeneas landed after his desperate flight from Troy (Virgil, *Aeneid*, Book III). And then, little by little, we arrive at our own day and age, by way of the Greeks, Romans, Byzantines, Normans, Swabians, Aragonese, Angevins, and Bourbons. A soul of different breeds, made up of people who have left their mark, visible in the dolmens, like the famous *Li Scusi* in the countryside near Minervino, in the menhirs, of which the town of Giurdignano preserves over fifteen examples, and in the *specchie*, large masses of conical stones up to thirty feet tall, such as the ones in Nardò, in the archeological parks of Rudiae and Roca Vecchia, all the way to the Byzantine mosaics of the church of Casaranello and the numerous defensive structures, bulwarks against the endless invasions.

But besides the history carved in the stones and the archeological ruins, there are many small towns in the hinterland—less well known than magical Lecce and the fairy-tale-like hamlets famous the world over, like Otranto, Gallipoli, and Ostuni—that still safeguard that rough popular courtesy, and have handed down stories of toil and land, sweat and hands, men and women who learned to survive on very little, and turn it into an epic poem. These are the places that serve as a backdrop to the dwellings in this book, like Nardò, a unique place with a rich history and monuments of great interest: a magnificent castle in a historical quarter that is completely and exclusively pedestrianized, numerous churches, and Baroque architecture that even Lecce would be envious of. And then there's the sea, over four miles of wild coastline, overhanging rock, twisting paths, watchtowers, and the karstic caves that form the Natural Regional Park of Porto Selvaggio and Palude del Capitano. An oasis of uncontaminated nature that stretches for an area of 2,800 acres, 1,067 of which are made up of coastline and 740 of which are occupied by pine groves.

In Marittima as well, the sea is king: located in between the hidden coves is Acquaviva, one of the most authentic gemstones of the Salento. This corner of the coastline, whose name comes from the fresh pools of spring water, with its steep cliffs and Mediterranean maquis shrubbery, is a living postcard, the very essence of a seaside vacation. The water, which is thermal here, rich in sulphur and minerals, is the hidden treasure of Santa Cesarea Terme as well, which over the years has become the preferred destination of the wealthy, who have come to own the villas in Moorish-style, so much so they look as though they belong to the opposite coast rather than to Salento's. The domes on the houses, especially Villa Sticchi, and the blue of the water, were chosen by the Italian actor Carmelo Bene—who is buried in the cemetery of Vitigliano—for the set of *Nostra Signora dei turchi*, the movie that won the Silver Lion at the Venice Film Festival in 1968.

Undoubtedly less noble, but no less fascinating, Giuggianello is one of the smallest of the towns in the province of Lecce. Though it isn't listed among the well-trodden tourist routes, it is an important stop from an archeological standpoint. A place that leaves room for the secrets of the stones, not only dolmens and menhirs but above all those peculiar large masses, the *furticiddhu della Vecchia*, hidden amid the olive trees, which have always fed into the popular imagination, and not just that. The treatise *On Marvelous Things Heard* (in the past attributed to Aristotle, its date is uncertain) is the first text to offer us some interesting information: the large stones were, according to ancient legend, the weapons that Hercules used during his epic battle against the Giants. His throws—the demigod was famous for his strength—were so powerful they reached all the way to Giuggianello, while the Giants, defeated and fallen into the sea, like therapeutic salts created the sulfurous water of Santa Cesarea, allegedly the site where the divine dispute took place. Popular culture then added a further magical touch, linking the masses to the "old woman," a witch and the wife of the much-feared Nanni Orcu.

Just twelve miles from Giuggianello, Depressa, a small suburb of Tricase, has a name that might sound a bit "depressing." There are some who say that it is a reminder of the offense suffered by the destruction wreaked by the Saracens, but it is more likely that it simply refers to the village's position, nestled in a natural depression in the earth. Hidden behind the somber irony of the name, however, is an aristocratic tale interwoven with the rural world. Here, the walls of Winspeare Castle and its austere fourteenth-century Angevin tower have become the favorite movie sets of Edoardo Winspeare, a cult film director and the owner, together with his brother, of this ancient fortress.

From prehistoric menhirs to thermal sites from the Roman age, from Byzantine church architecture to refined examples of the Baroque and to aristocratic palazzi of the nineteenth century, Bagnolo del Salento also offers a journey across the layers of history. At one time famous for the artisanal production of rope, which earned the people there the nickname of *zuccari* (rope-makers), today it still wears its special attire made of Leccese stone, in between Baroque clues and Byzantine nuances.

Just a few miles from the town is the hamlet of Cannole, one of thirteen in the area of Otranto that have preserved the traditions and language from the distant past when it was under Greek rule. In addition to the castle, Baroque churches, famous *masserie*, and menhirs, not far from the center of town nature offers its own spectacle as well: the Alimini salt lakes, close to the Adriatic Sea. Spongano is another small village that has recently become a tourist destination; its attractions include an underground olive press, hidden in the cellars of Palazzo Bacile di Castiglione, declared to be of art-historical interest by the Soprintendenza per i Beni

Architettonici e Paesaggistici. Used from the seventeenth century to the mid-1950s, it is the first in the Basso Salento dedicated to the "industrial" production of edible oil. And then there's Salve, just a stone's throw away from Santa Maria di Leuca, which, in addition to its famous marinas—Pescoluse, Torre Pali, Posto Vecchio, and Lido Marini—has one of the oldest working organs in Italy, in the church of San Nicola Magno, underneath vaults decorated with precious eighteenth-century stuccowork.

But as we get to the end of this short tale, we simply must mention Lecce—known as the "Florence of Puglia"—with its aristocratic allure and unsurpassable Middle Eastern charm. Its residences and churches tell the story of the stratification of many epochs up until the apotheosis of the Baroque, its dominant signature style. Palaces that are absolute gemstones like Carrelli-Palombi, featuring enchanting single lancet windows, and Tamborino Cezzi, with its Wunderkammer, living proof of this glorious past, immortalized by Ferzan Ozpetek in the movies *Fasten Your Seatbelts* and *Loose Cannons*. Aesthetic perfection is achieved in the ecclesiastical architecture here, like the Duomo, which exhibits its facades like a steadfast bulwark of faith in praise of the Assumption of Mary, and sanctions the new legend of Saint Orontius of Lecce, proclaimed the patron saint of the city in 1658. Lastly, there's Otranto, a splendid city overlooking the Adriatic Sea, and the farthest to the east in Italy. Indeed, a few miles from here, Punta Palascia holds the easternmost geographical position in all of Italy. On cloudless days, from the Canale d'Otranto, the stretch of sea that separates Italy from Albania, one can clearly see the Albanian coast on the horizon, and imagine the two countries were waving to each other. The area also hosts an abandoned bauxite quarry, now filled by a lake with emerald green water.

Sea and country, rural and aristocratic architecture, Salento with its heart always open is ready to welcome those who know how to listen, to see beyond the mirage, because they know the value of every journey, of every return. Without ever having to say farewell.

---

[1] *Masseria* comes from *massaro*, the person who ran the farming estate, from the Latin *massa*: "land ownership," "asset."
[2] Guido Piovene, *Viaggio in Italia* (Milan: Bompiani, 1957), 608.
[3] Cesare Brandi, *Pellegrino di Puglia* (Rome: Editori Riuniti, 2004), 31.
[4] Pier Paolo Pasolini, *La lunga strada di sabbia* (Milan: Guanda, 2014), 150.

SPONGANO

if one day a female traveler

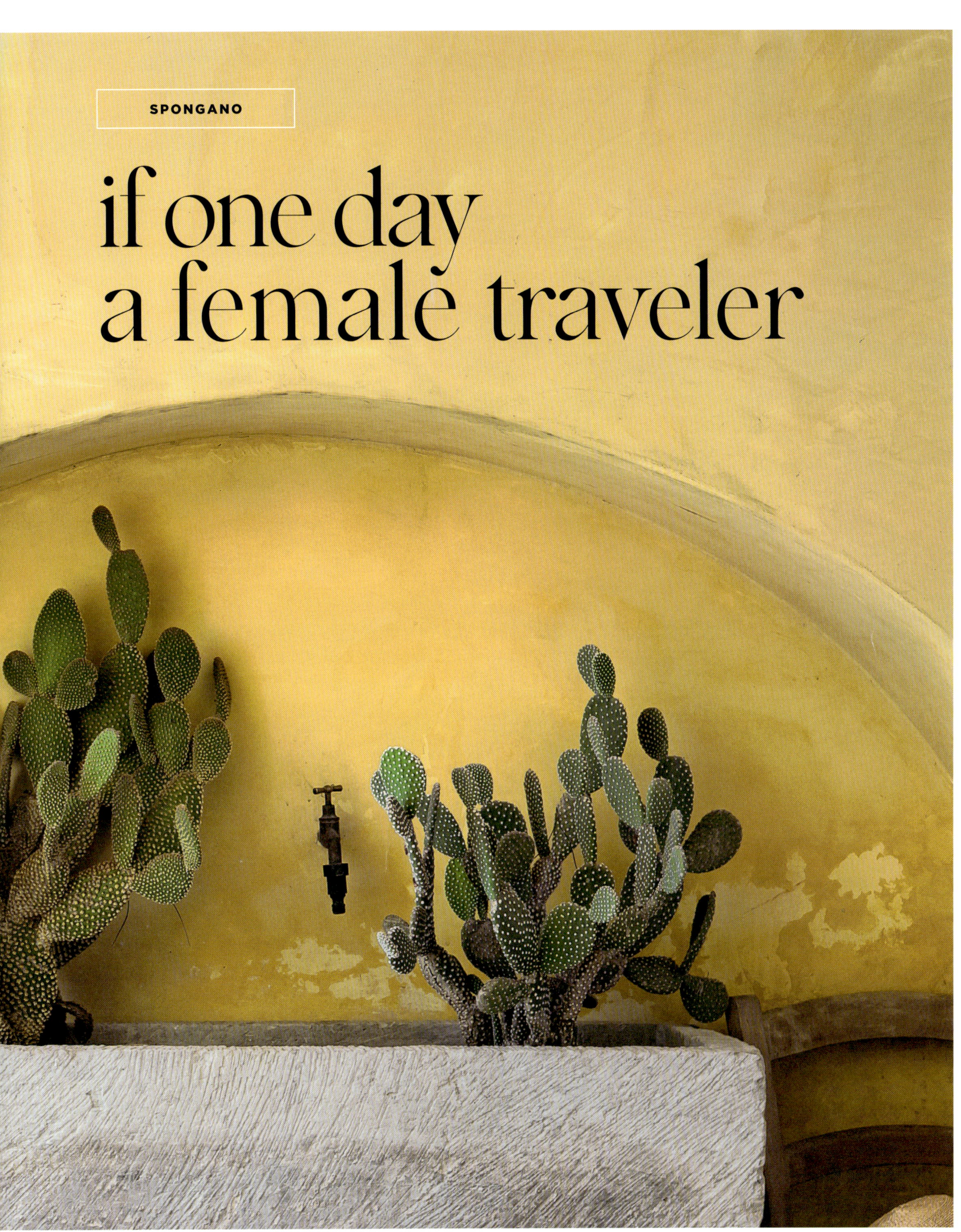

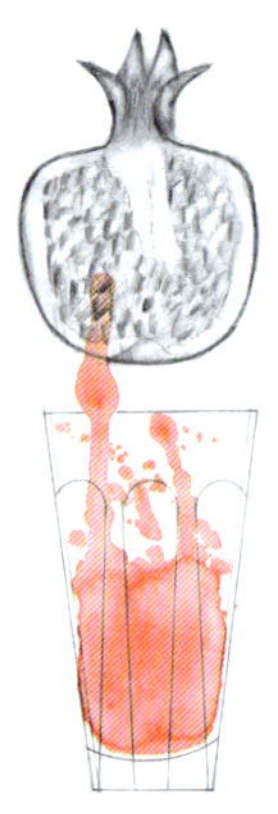

A land that invites, envelops,
and then gently holds.
For many, it is rugged, harsh,
and all-embracing, yet
overflowing with soul.
A land whose complexity
has always drawn an
endless crossroads
of peoples, who have settled
here and planted thick,
tangled, and profound roots.

SPONGANO

1. A VILLAGE HOME HIDDEN BEHIND AN ANCIENT DOOR

A land that still today welcomes anyone who sets foot on it with a familiar embrace, evoking a sense of *déjà vu* and immediately awakening a deep feeling of belonging. Nothing forced, though. In Salento, life is lived by choice. That is what happened to Francesca Marciano—a globe-trotting screenwriter who realized in New York that she wanted to be a writer—who arrived in the land of Otranto without even being acquainted with it. Repeatedly invited by a friend, she had always hesitated: the long and difficult train journey from Rome, where she now lives, seemed daunting, even for someone like her, used to having her bags always packed. Then one day, thirty years ago, luggage in hand, she accepted the invitation, set off for Salento, and discovered the region and the beauty of Lecce, with its masterful chromatic solo made of stone. A world away from New York's skyline, where she had lived for years, and from the boundless landscapes of Kenya, her second adopted home, which she had sadly left during that period of transition.

"Puglia is the heel of Italy, the thinnest strip of land between two seas. Lorenzo, my grandfather, said it was exactly this—the refraction of the sun hitting the water on both sides—that made the light of Puglia so rich and warm." These are Alina's words—the female voice of the novel *Casa Rossa*, written by Francesca during that very period—recounting what Lorenzo, the protagonist's grandfather, said when he decided to lay down roots in this borderland. The book was originally supposed to be set in Sicily, but in the end, Salento won. A double victory, or perhaps a twist of fate, because Francesca also let down her guard on that occasion. After a period of renting homes in the small province, she made the same choice: not a luxury farmhouse with a pool—she needed to be in the village among the people, just a few miles from the sea, because early-morning swimming is her great passion. A casual tour of Spongano with a friend, organized almost as a whim, turned into love at first sight: by the third visit, it was the house that found her. Simple and not too large for one person, the rural home that won her over had something unique compared with the others—it held a story waiting to be told. Nothing written, of course, just village whispers and a few clues etched into the stone, all hints that, when listened to, interpreted, and described, transform into silent narratives. And in hindsight, there couldn't have been a more fitting place for a talented writer like Francesca, renowned for her novels, written in English and translated into fifteen languages (including Italian, of course), and for her unforgettable screenplays for directors such as Bernardo Bertolucci, Cristina Comencini, Nanni Moretti, Gabriele Salvatores, and Carlo Verdone, to name just a few. Not to mention her latest work with Valeria Golino, *The Art of Joy*, which brought to the screen the complex posthumous novel by Goliarda Sapienza.

Inside these walls, however, there is no best-selling story waiting to come out. Here, the plot is much simpler: an elderly widow, considered by many in the village to be a bit mean, who, despite her humble origins, had clearly married well—as proven not only by the donkey but also by the horse she owned. A self-aware peasant woman who placed a grape coat of arms above the front door—not as a pretentious display of nobility, but more likely as a simple reference to a valuable vineyard she owned nearby. But the real mystery of the house lies in one detail: a rounded, smoothly

1.

worn indentation in the *chianche* floor (a very old type of stone paving typical of the area) on the first floor. At first glance, it might seem like just a mark left by time, but in reality, it is an unresolved enigma that still today adds charm and mystery to the house.

The late-nineteenth-century structure has been preserved by its owner as it was—a perfect example of historical architecture oozing the charm of a bygone era. With the help of her architect friend Stefania Miscetti, Francesca made very few changes to the building: where the upstairs kitchen once was, she created a double bathroom, enhancing functionality without altering the home's essence. The result is an architecture that feels almost austere, both inside and out, in harmony with the rural constructions of the area. A light touch that reflects a deep respect for the natural surroundings and the region's heritage, creating a continuous dialogue of references and overlays. Few modifications were made: an extra window and a second bathroom on the ground floor—just essential upgrades. The rest still retains that old-world flavor, including the stone-clad courtyard facade leading to the house, weathered by time, punctuated by yellow walls and windows painted a delicate aqua green. A wooden door, never renovated—so much so that for a long time many in the village thought the house was still uninhabited—a small courtyard, two above-ground floors, and a large garden thus became Francesca's secret kingdom, tucked away among other homes.

The small entrance courtyard is enlivened by an external staircase, arches, raised levels, and a stone sink, creating a playful contrast with the rear facade—linear and fresh, with large openings overlooking

the garden. The entrance once housed donkeys and horses but has now been transformed into a spacious, elegantly furnished living area. A pair of retro-inspired striped sofas warmly welcome anyone stepping inside. The thick white-plastered walls and star-shaped vaulted ceilings offer a refuge from the relentless heat, preserving the interior's coolness. From here, a sequence of rooms leads toward the greenery of the garden: a large open-plan kitchen with a dining table, a bathroom cleverly concealed within a double closet with sliding doors, and a veranda painted a delicate green—all flowing harmoniously toward the outdoors. Fresh air circulates from the courtyard, naturally connecting with the rear garden area. Here, a small concrete staircase leads upstairs, where large arched windows frame a romantic view of an old almond tree. In this space, a second veranda—enriched with mementos from the writer's African past and Indian touches mixed with local crafts—becomes the starting point for exploring the other rooms. Among them is the large double bathroom, created in the space that once served as the kitchen. This former heart of the home still features its fireplace and *fornacelle*—stone-cut compartments once used as primitive cooking surfaces fueled by burning coals from the adjacent fire. Essential for preparing simple, economical family meals, these relics have now been transformed into practical bathroom shelves, preserving a sense of the past while catering to modern needs. A series of rooms follows: a sitting room, bedroom, and study overlooking the inner courtyard—all airy spaces painted in soft pastel hues, transitioning from a warm pearly tone to an ethereal blue in the sleeping area, and a mossy green in the bathroom. The furnishings, plain yet thoughtfully curated, are pieces gathered over time—salvaged from other homes or purchased at local markets—woven into this space to create a deeply personal and intimate world. Every item carries a story, a memory, or an emotional connection, fragments of life that tell of journeys, discoveries, experiences, and chance.

The rear of the house, with its well-proportioned facade, fully opens onto the greenery through two rows of windows, both flat and arched, on the upper floor. The garden, bordered by traditional dry-stone walls, follows the custom of Salentine homes, hosting a pomegranate tree, an orange tree, a lemon tree, and an old almond tree that still bears fruit despite its age. And, of course, flowers—narcissus blooming in March, radiant roses in May. As the seasons change, Francesca's connection to Spongano has grown ever stronger. Every excuse—even a change in sea temperature—becomes a reason to return to this land that claimed her heart long ago. Thanks to her career as a writer, she now spends much of the year in Salento. She, like many other women drawn toward this sincere embrace, follows a journey unbound by geography or maps, guided instead by the rhythms of the heart. Her home has become a personal novel, with life's pages shaped by the rhythm of time, pauses of silence, and authentic beauty found in small gestures. It's a journey in search of deeper truths, where remaining in itself becomes a destination already written about.

1.

*One of the many mementos of the trips taken by the lady of the house.
To the right, the minimalist, large concrete bathtub
has a place to itself under a vault painted sage,
creating an intimate atmosphere suspended in time.*

*On the door, a sacred heart portraying Frida Kahlo.
To the left, the series of rooms on the first floor is slowly unveiled,
with the bedroom and the studio one after the other, in a continuing
and harmonious dialogue between intimacy and creative space.*

1.

Jean Gaumy, the photographer and film-maker, grew
up close to the Bay of Biscay and now lives in
Fecamp, the port from where France's cod fleet once
set out for the Newfoundland fishing grounds. He
has sailed with several fishing fleets. His pictures on
the following pages come from two voyages: here,
and on the eight pages beginning overleaf, with a
Spanish crew line-fishing for tuna; on subsequent
pages, aboard another Spanish boat trawling in
the Atlantic and the North Sea.

GIUGGIANELLO

toward another place

Discretion and anonymity seem to be the rule in this part of Salento, but at times reality can be deceptive: there is much more than meets the eye in the streets of Giuggianello, one of the smallest towns in the province of Lecce.

GIUGGIANELLO

2. A VILLAGE DWELLING
A SECRET GARDEN IN A TREASURE TROVE

And by that we don't mean the famous botanical garden La Cutura, which is set inside an ancient *masseria* just a few miles from the town, and hosts one of the richest collections of cacti, and tropical and Mediterranean plants in all of Europe. We mean a *magione* that is reserved, intimate, and unique in its kind. A house among many accessible from a secondary road, bordered by buildings that might seem to have no character at first, with facades in dull colors and doors left ajar to let the air in and thus defeat the unbearable summer heat. Although they may look as though they were slumbering in the sun, showing no apparent sign of life, something escapes you at first glance.

"An invisible landscape conditions the visible one; everything that moves in the sunlight is driven by the lapping wave enclosed beneath the rock's calcareous sky," wrote Italo Calvino.[1] There is an intimate, modest discretion that one discovers only after knocking on a door that, once opened, reveals the unexpected. A universe that is immediately seen as a crossroads of lives and worlds and that cannot hide the homeowners' passion for culture and beauty.

Peter Benson Miller, an art historian and formerly the artistic director of the American Academy in Rome, with numerous publications to his name and a new book about to be published, along with Giovanni Panebianco, President of the Premio Paganini, an international contest for young violinists in Genoa: these two intellectuals uncontrollably attracted to beauty have decided to "cultivate" their garden here. An American—and a Roman by choice for over thirty years—and a Calabrian, who, in their long trips to the Middle East, have amassed collections that range from Syrian glass to Anatolian fabrics, mixed in with lots of "souvenirs d'Italie" (especially ceramics from Sicily, Vietri, and Albissola), now perfectly integrated in the aesthetics of their home in Salento. Before falling in love with this small part of the world, they were looking for their "other place," a place where they could stop and exhibit all the pieces that they—especially Peter—had collected. They found their match in this far-flung land that the ancient Romans called *Finis Terrae* (the World's End), with its many layers of history, witness to the passage of Greeks, Romans, Normans, and Ottomans. A land that welcomes everyone, still today, a destination for the soul that for many requires a profound process of initiation.

The search began in the fall of 2007 and, after several attempts, it was focused right here, in a village that is known to only a few, and that can be reached by streets geometrically designed by dry walls that were at one time studded with olive trees that now suffer. But nature is not always tyrannical; actually, in Giuggianello it can be generous. Such as in this dwelling, which harbors one of the most luxuriant corners of greenery in the area, covered with copious vegetation, including tangerine, bitter orange, fig, and pomegranate trees. The plan for the house seems to have been orchestrated so that it would relate to the luxuriant flora of the garden, in a constant ebbing and flowing and whispering of the air. You get a sense of it as soon as you cross the large entrance hall covered with a traditional star-shaped vault, an area that at one time must have been destined to everyday toil, seeing the width of the vehicle entrance overlooking the street.

As you enter, two gazes on opposite walls immediately catch your attention: on one side is a painting of Garibaldi, a gift from a friend, and on the other is the portrait of an illustrious Dragoman—the ancient figure of the translator, the person who served as a bridge for political and cultural relations between the West and the Middle East—purchased in a Parisian market, instantly establishing that dialogue between worlds that is the key to understanding this couple's passions.

In the broad space of the atrium we can still feel the history of the building that, at the time of purchase, was divided into two almost equal parts without a true rationale, in order to fulfill the needs of an inheritance between brothers. Dust, walls roughly plastered over, spaces to be reconquered. And yet, between the thick walls, Peter and Giovanni instantly understood that there was a story to pick up once more, starting from an *incipit*, a first line, worthy of an epic novel: the colored tiles from the late nineteenth century, decorated with fancy floral and geometric motifs, saved almost miraculously from the "cuts" of time. Which led to the idea of having all the rooms converse with one another through those characteristic designs, and also fill in the gaps due to the house's previous life. But the project immediately proved to be more complex than was expected: the old tiles found by the local retailers were not enough. It was fate that was a game-changer: during a vacation near Byblos, in Lebanon, in 2008, they discovered a warehouse filled with 1920s tiles, perfect for their home, and, quite by chance, originally from Italy. There were enough of them to fulfill their needs, and were thus used to create "carpets," each one different, and as if in pursuit of each other from one room to the next.

The refurbishment brought to light other genuine architectural treasures: a courtyard in the local Leccese stone, with hand-cut slabs the color of honey, and two carved arches, probably the remains of the Venetian and Middle Eastern colonizers who, between the seventeenth and eighteenth centuries, had decreed Salento to be the crossroads of trade. A fragment of time that joins the living room to the kitchen, two Gothic portals—a *coup de théâtre*—that with their presence transform this space into the heart of the house. The large French windows that open onto the garden, embraced by the wisteria in this season without flowers, complete the atmosphere. The kitchen, which is entirely built in masonry, features a terrazzo floor and walls finished in vintage Carrara marble found in Lebanon, like many of the other materials used for the house's refurbishment.

From the large space with arches, furnished with a library filled with artbooks and a Pantheon dining table designed by Mario Bellini for Cassina (no longer produced), one enters a sitting room—an absolute *cabinet d'amateur*—with a fireplace and a sofa bought at an auction in Genoa: Peter believes it is the best auction to do business. On the wall is one of the "pieces" the couple loves the most; a painting bought in a garage in Hama portraying the ancient Syrian city. They agreed on their purchase right away: Peter, who is always enthusiastic about any new object to add to their various collections, and Giovanni, who tries to rein him in. And now that it hangs on the wall, it has become a nostalgic tribute to beauty that has vanished, a fragment of memory that survives notwithstanding a war that has obfuscated that happily fertile landscape.

After also buying a smaller house next-door, and opening up a courtyard between the two, the couple began interweaving paths to enhance the rooms overlooking the greenery. They worked by subtraction, freeing up the space to build the bright and airy atmosphere that characterizes the house today. After the daytime area, three rooms with four-poster beds and two

bathrooms run all along the perimeter of the garden. At the back, a small internal courtyard that is reminiscent of a luxuriant riyad leads to the upper floor of the residence via an outdoor stairway. A house-inside-a-house, a private place—the bedroom has a four-poster bed, and there's a bathroom with a tub made of cast-iron, a small sitting room, and a *studiolo*—that overlooks the road below and gathers up, besides the breeze, all the town gossip. Walking from one room to another, the air we breathe is steeped in a sophisticated aesthetic research, a tangible manifestation of the owners' passion and curiosity, the tale in episodes of an intimate and ongoing trip through beauty and culture. For Peter and Giovanni, even though they don't always agree on purchases, do not limit themselves to collecting objects. Rather, they accumulate memories and dreams as well, and have transformed their home into a treasure trove of affection and things they want to remember, a deep expression of their shared identity. For collecting is not just a passion, but—especially for Peter, accustomed ever since he was a child to wandering around markets and antiques shops with his parents—a necessity. Their treasures include a collection of painter's palettes, found between Paris and Rome, that now adorn the wall in the small sitting room. And it should come as no surprise that next to a twentieth-century Italian desk is an American Windsor chair, or that in one of the guest rooms eighteenth-century Southern Italian votive elements are mounted above a rustic nineteenth-century French bed. The periods in history blend together seamlessly here. The sitting room, library, bedrooms, and bathrooms tell us of a never-ending search for the rare piece, often accompanied by contemporary decor, such as the lamps signed Michele De Lucchi. Wherever you look you see ceramics of various provenance, proof of Peter's passion; he began molding clay when he was a young boy. Soon a new studio with a kiln beyond the garden will be added to this already elaborate *magione*, further expanding this intriguing domestic universe.

And then there's the art, a constant throughout the house, which offers a counterpoint to the vintage elements with contemporary touches of the living artists whom Peter admires. These include the sculptures of F. Taylor Colantonio, Namsal Siedlecki, and Tomaso De Luca in the sitting room, a bronze bust by Leonid Lerman in the garden, and the glass sculpture by Tristano di Robilant, sitting prettily on the dining room table. Not to mention several drawings with a Bic pen by Giuseppe Stampone, a painting by Viola Yesiltac in the living room, and the small canvases by Dawn Kasper, the vestige of a performance at the American Academy in 2016.

Peter also designed the outdoor terraces, transforming the landscape into a harmonious interweaving of nature and architecture. He created paths bordered by elegant Agapanthus plants and fragrant roses, a dense garden of aromatic and Mediterranean herbs, and, at the far end of the green expanse, a narrow pool that is elevated, a gemstone of water inspired by the vats in Middle Eastern gardens. Another passageway toward that other place that has by now grown so close, a place of potential expressed in the present.

[1] Italo Calvino, *Invisible Cities* (London: Vintage Books, 1997), 17.

The large living room combines vintage pieces like Marcel Breuer's Wassily armchairs with contemporary artworks.
To the left, the rooms on the ground floor feature vintage cement tiles with geometric patterns, discovered during a trip.

A corner of the dining room with a painting, a family heirloom, surrounded by several pieces from the couple's collection of antique ceramics. To the right, the vintage table and chairs converse with the large interwoven sculpture by F. Taylor Colantonio.

*A detail from the collection of ex-votos decorating the guest bathroom on the ground floor.
To the right, the masonry kitchen, characterized by clean lines
and traditional materials, lit by the metal lamps designed by Michele De Lucchi.*

2.

DU ROYAUME DE POLOGNE

The bathroom on the upper floor, with a large cast-iron bathtub, bought at an antiques market, at the center. To the right, the opposite side of the same room, entirely finished in vintage Carrara marble bought on a trip to Lebanon.

*The small inner courtyard, completely made of Leccese stone, grows luxuriantly,
and brings air to the rooms on the ground floor.
To the left, the stone tub, finished with tiles featuring arabesque motifs,
bestows a Middle Eastern accent on the whole.*

CANNOLE

back to the fold

Fade out, transition.
The scene changes: no town
in sight, just the countryside
playing the leading role.
A slow landscape, where time
seems to have made a deal
with the land, a place where
the olive trees, the ancient
guardians, some of them
reduced to leafless skeletons
by Xylella, have branches
that lift upward like arms
outstretched in a gesture
of pleading but not surrender.

CANNOLE

3. A HOUSE THAT WAS ONCE A SHEEPFOLD

AN ART WORKSHOP CRADLED BY OLIVE TREES

The dry walls, built stone on stone, follow the outline of the land like veins crossing the skin of this region. The sun high in the sky grants no respite, it is the absolute master, burning mercilessly, but also giving these fields brighter colors, more clearly outlined shadows. Here, near Cannole, a town five miles from Otranto, modernity, at least for now, is still an outsider. Just wilderness, where the soul awakens to its fate and art is fused with life, slowly melding with nature, step by step, like walking down the wooden runway that spreads from one building to the next in this hamlet.

This house—which was once a sheepfold—albeit of modest dimensions, encompasses the entire world of its owner, Michele Sambin, a musician, painter, filmmaker, and pioneer of video-art, who, from the early 1970s, forced himself to go beyond the limits of experimentation to combine several disciplines: cinema, music, painting, and, lastly, theater, which he found to be the place of synthesis. Born in Padua, with a past that is lost in the maze of Venice's artistic avant-garde—where the Galleria del Cavallino served as a lighthouse for visionaries—he has always been capable of strumming the invisible chords of the imagination (as well as of his cello). A pioneer, a dream-catcher, who with his Tam Teatromusica, together with Pierangela Allegro and Laurent Dupont, has woven together patterns of sounds, images, and words, not as the simple lines of a musical score but as a unique and unrepeatable song. His past, consumed by the haste and passion typical of bygone times, has now found a new purity amid the everyday frames, where repetition—or rather a loop, for he who is an expert in digital art—becomes a ritual and time expands.

This is not a tale that toys with fate, it is not a rhythm that bows down to the inevitable. After crossing Italy, traveling down many roads with his theater company, Michele found Salento to be a place in which to stop, a small corner of a world immersed in the countryside, close to one of those thirteen towns in the heel of Italy where ancient words in Greek blend in with the local dialect. It is here that he chose to lay down roots, far from the din, amid the traditions of a language from a past that stubbornly lives on, with a forgotten melody that resurfaces with the wind. A conscious choice, for in the land of Otranto, besides the savage beauty of nature, he found the kindness that makes the Salentine people extraordinary. A return to the fold, not for those who seek forgiveness but for those who have rediscovered that there is more space for creativity in nature that is wild, primitive. A discovery that smacks of a conquest, like Michele's home, which you don't see right away but that appears like a small fortress carefully hidden between the stone walls, the trees, and the greenery all around.

The entrance is at the rear, and to go inside you have to take a short walk. The structure is not subject to any logical design. It is by nature a performance of creativity. A garden with orange trees and olive trees that protrude beyond the veranda and that Michele has turned into instruments for an imaginary string orchestra in a "natural" guise. Structures to provide shade, blocks of stone, and circles of gravel as if the Far East had magically decided to change its geographical coordinates and head toward the Mediterranean. But nothing was planned beforehand, even Japan was already present, all you had to do was look for it among the large "cuti" (jutting rocks) emerging from the terrain inside the house and in the vegetation integrated with the architecture. Everything—except for a building that was added on later—was already this way. All that needed to be done was to listen to and go along with that rural area as if it were a work in progress, and help it with internal and external scores, sliding panels and hinged windows, so that nature was insinuated with discretion and the trees became one with the house, thus creating a harmonious conversation between inside and outside, just like in the Land of Cherry Blossoms. This vision is not born from any direct experience with the land of the Rising Sun, but from imagination and inspiration. Like Salgari, who knew how to use vivid words to paint far-flung places like the islands of Malaysia or the kingdom of the Corsairs without ever having set foot there, Sambin as well was able to evoke the beauty of that distant country without ever having actually visited it. He did so through poetic, sensitive synthesis, a vision that, albeit without direct experience, manages to capture the essence of those places and convey their mystery and beauty in a voice all its own. An intense story that, even without being able to boast about a noble origin—the sheepfold here does not have a centuries-old, aristocratic history behind it—brings with it the secret of another dimension.

No star-shaped vaults, no cement tiles, the building built after World War Two was conceived for practical purposes: fresh ricotta every day to fulfill the morning wishes of the former owner of the land and the nearby aristocratic dwelling. In time, that space went on to change its inhabitants: in addition to two new shepherds, chickens accompanied by other barnyard animals arrived as well. A rural vocation that was not forgotten by the current owner: still today the entrance to the house is known as the "recinto agnelli" (lamb pen), in memory of when they were weaned here. This dwelling, in its purest essence, still preserves the sign of ancient times with its humble organization of spaces and its Leccese stone walls: on the one hand, a dining room, on the other, a simple pallet, a shelter for the dreams of those who worked the land and took the flocks out to pasture. Michele, with a light hand and the help of the local craftsmen, added only a bathroom, without upsetting the balance of a place conceived for art and that continues to thrive on art.

The interior decor, which is spartan with a sober and sincere orderliness, speaks of simplicity that accentuates the harmony of the whole. The daytime area, with a small kitchen featuring a cleverly hidden stovetop, has a fireplace, a table, and a sofa that together encourage conviviality. Next to that, separated by sliding walls, is a minimalist bedroom with a large-scale painting titled *Anime gemelle*—a reference to the artist's art and life with his wife Pierangela—crowned by a blue ceiling that would appear to be competing with the firmament. The contrast in this environment almost seems "photographic," with the white reflecting the light and the black absorbing it. Very few colors were used in the dwelling, most of them chosen based on the nature of the place, except for that patch of lapis lazuli blue that emerges from the artist's paintings and in between the walls of the rooms. This is Michele's favorite color, reminiscent of the famous shade that Yves Klein would use for his *Monochromes*, but also recalling the skies of Giotto's Scrovegni Chapel in his birthplace. A shade that triumphs in what is referred to as the "blue room," a corner of pure inspiration

covered by a transparent roof that filters light in the manner of an ethereal veil, with a large table fastened to the wall, which can be detached and mounted with a simple, mechanically fluid gesture whenever needed.

This is Michele's realm, a creative sanctuary where the artist takes refuge in the half-seasons, finding the peace and inspiration he needs to bring his works to life. All the wooden furniture in the house is not only made by hand but built by the artist himself. He imbues each piece with the same passion with which he paints or plays the cello. Michele's art inside this home is just whispered, a delicate tale that traces the essential stages of his creative trajectory. Like the photographic sequence of his most significant video, *Il tempo consuma (1978/2022)*, which crosses the wall from the daytime to the nighttime area, forcing us to look up as we walk toward the bedroom. Or the work from 1970 titled *Obra roja*, "created in pieces" so that the user can invent their own personal composition, which stands out above the sofa. But the magic does not end here: throughout the house each element is ready to be transformed, to respond to the needs of art, which is tantamount to life.

The furnishings, like restless souls, bend to the will of time, changing form and meaning, spurred by wheels and gears telling stories that change each day. It is precisely there, where the bleating of the sheep could be heard in what was once the barn, that we find the heart of a subtle magic, a curtainless theater, where alchemy comes to life. The setting is a simple one: a ceiling with white-painted wooden beams, a row of windows up at the top, concrete on the floor, a few jutting rocks that peer out from the wall, and, for the lighting, a series of music stands, the ones typically used by musicians, which, transformed into lamps, illuminate the scene as at a concert. It is a multipurpose space, able to serve as a stage for a performance, a sartorial workshop, or a lab for those who know how to make things from nothing. A world that oozes change, where every corner is an invitation for the imagination to thrive, a place where art is combined with life, revealing with every gaze a new facet in that mystery we call creativity. Outside, lying in between the furrows in the earth, there is also a hut—a space built for Pierangela, a small studio for her art, a microcosm that takes shape and substance from nature, in perfect harmony with it. There, in that silent corner, the leafless branches of the olive trees become columns and supports, entwining with the wisteria until they become an embrace of light and shadow, where the straight lines merge with the free forms of nature. Parallel universes in between luxuriant and suffering nature, where even the canvas awnings strive, with great effort, to dominate the powerful sunlight. The result of this is an image veiled by a subtle melancholy, which also becomes a cure-all that helps the healing. This is the story that is told in the documentary *Più de la vita,* directed by Raffaella Rivi, set in Padua and Salento, in which Sambin, who plays himself, explains his art like a modern-day Ruzante—a sixteenth-century Italian playwright—who in his final letter-cum-testament reflects on the importance of a life that must be lived with awareness and intensity: profound more than lengthy. And perhaps lived amid the walls of a sheepfold, which for Michele was never like a farewell to the world, but a fresh start, a path toward boundless creativity. A utopia that, day after day, becomes reality only here.

A detail of the olive tree that has been affected by Xylella and has been transformed into a string instrument. To the right, the "cuti"–rocks jutting out from the ground–that characterize the floor in what was once a stable, and suggest a Japanese tone for the house.

3.

yeast
Il gatto
Albert Camus Maria Casarès
SAREMO LEGGERI

MICHELE SAMBIN

3.

On the previous pages, two views of the bedroom with a blue ceiling, separated from the living room by sliding walls. Above a simple, almost basic bed, the painting Anime gemelle, *a reference to the artist's art and life with his wife Pierangela.*

Below, a number of photographic sequences from the video Il tempo consuma (1978/2022). *To the right, the living room with fireplace. The decor is simple, and hanging on the wall above the sofa is the painting* Obra roja, *1970.*

STAMPO
CAPPELLO

The work àbitat, *by Pierangela Allegro,*
placed inside the atelier built for her by her husband.
To the right, sculptures-objects Salvati dal fuoco,
made by Michele Sambin with recycled pieces.

A view of the atelier created for Pierangela by Michele amid olive branches and wisteria, interwoven in an embrace of light and shadow. To the left, the artist's work table in the atelier devoted to her, with panels opening onto nature outside.

the theater of the world

Ponti
BIZARRE
Patrick Caulfield Paintings
Peter Blake
RODIN BRANCUSI MOORE
SENSATION
TAPLIN
La Colombe d'Or
Marella Agnelli The Last Swan
RICHARD LONG
RICHARD LONG
RICHARD LONG

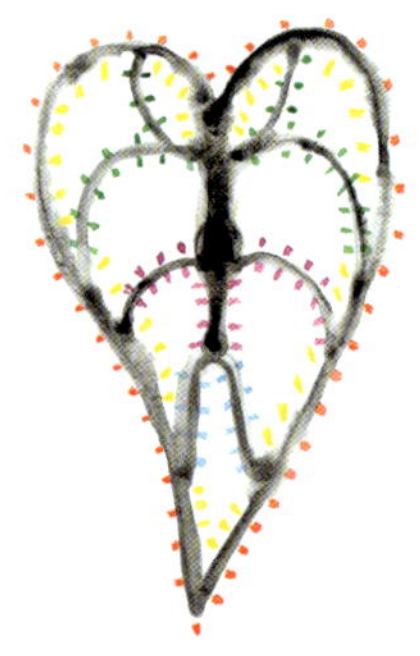

The walls, albeit very thick and imposing, cannot hide the secret they enclose. The clues aren't many—a few windows protected by grates, no concession to decor, and next to it a small seventeenth-century church. And yet, in the silence of the countryside surrounding the building that is at times gentle and at others bitter, you instantly sense the echo of ancient prayer lost over the centuries.

MARITTIMA

4. **THE FORMER CONVENT OF SANTA MARIA DI COSTANTINOPOLI**
FLOWERS AND SCULPTURES AMAZE GUESTS

This is Marittima, in the province of Lecce—just a few miles from Acquaviva, an inlet almost hidden from the large cliffs looming directly over the sea—and behind the large door is the Convent of Santa Maria di Costantinopoli, a site where at every step all you discern is the summoning of the soul, while time seems to be suspended. No sign, not even a doorbell, just the number on the door telling you that concealed behind these mighty "bastions" is a place of rest, an intimate and informal guest house that resembles more of a house than a conventional hotel. But there's nothing strange here. Already in the early centuries of the past millennium, wayfarers would find a bed for the night right below these star-shaped vaults, and so we shouldn't be surprised that it is once again a place where modern travelers can find hospitality. Built in the fourteenth century, it has undergone several changes, and when the Franciscan community that lived there was permanently expelled, it became first a tobacco factory and then a shelter for livestock and farming machinery.

Until 1997, that is, when Alistair McAlpine, a maverick English lord, fell in love with these dilapidated walls, and recognized the great potential of this strange and powerful corner of Puglia. But for his dream to come true there had to be something else: it was the insight of his last wife, Athena, of Greek origin, an independent soul who still today, now that her husband has passed away, continues, alone, to walk barefoot down the long hallways. Two free and cosmopolitan spirits, thirsty for knowledge, who together turned this place into a life experience. Their own. Their world and their soul are here, generously bestowed on today's pilgrims through the stories of the eight rooms, all of them different, chock-full of objects and paintings, not to mention the myriad ethnic fabrics and books piled up everywhere. And to think that at one time half of the complex was in ruins and the garden was completely overgrown... It took five years between works and complicated authorizations, to get it back into shape, and another four to create that concerto of plants and flowers that is now an Eden where the lady of the house enjoys working.

Here you can breathe culture and passion everywhere. It could not be otherwise: McAlpine, a generous man with a panoply of interests—politician, builder, journalist, writer—was a famous collector who seemed to want to encompass the universe in a closet. An extreme undertaking. Athena knows this well. Obstinate and exacting in her ways, over the years she has inventoried everything—the way the ancient monks once did; they did not just copy and transcribe texts, but annotated them, conserving them carefully in the monastic libraries—so as to maintain and preserve with love the spirit of this sophisticated, free, and nonconformist place. Berber carpets, African sculptures, tribal masks, and many other things in a context of bold, lively colors, seem to adapt perfectly to the rough walls made of the local stone in this ancient place of worship. Just as in the outdoor space, a half-English-, half-Italian-style garden, there is a mixture of shapes and colors that combine and separate to the soul's delight. It seems like the collection of a lifetime, also because of the sheer number of pieces, which could fill a whole museum. But the truth of the matter is that the collection assembled by the couple was only the last of many. The objects are thus an anthology that describes their life more than any written page, as if behind an Ethiopian mask—to borrow the words of the philosopher, writer, and great collector Walter Benjamin— there was a sort of "magic encyclopedia."[1]

A theater of the world that is instantly revealed after crossing the threshold: especially in the summertime, you immediately perceive a pleasant change in temperature and the red of the walls is both disorienting and intriguing. On the walls, carved faces, ceremonial effigies, and historical marionettes from Mali welcome visitors, while the silence of the cloister is disrupted solely by the chirping of the swallows, regular residents of the Convent for many summers now. Under the vaults is a pot-pourri of Ashanti chairs and stools typical of Niger, heaps of ethnic pillows, and antique inlaid tables from Ethiopia.

The square plan of the cloister distributes, in addition to the rooms on the ground floor, a series of living areas of various sizes, a common dining room with a large table, a kitchen open to all overlooking the garden, and, separately, a professional-looking laundry room. The decor—perhaps too formal a word for a place where informality is the rule—is a trip around the world that does not require an app on your smartphone to get your bearings. In fact, technology is banned here: the rooms have no air-conditioning, there is no trace of a minibar (the fridge in the kitchen is always open to all), there's no telephone, just as there is no TV, but instead there are forty tons of books—which are hard to avoid because they truly are everywhere and freely available.

In this dwelling a surprise always lies just around the corner, amid paintings hung on the walls, jars neatly arranged, and a variety of objects that generate a strange emotional geography, fluttering between the meanders of memories and emotions.

The effect of it being too full—always a risk in cases such as these—is carefully avoided as passion here follows its own metric everywhere, just as poetry does. There is a constant attempt to bring order to where disorder reigns, "nothing more than a hovering over the abyss"[2]—to quote Walter Benjamin once again—in the scene of one's own destiny. Each thing reveals itself to be the bearer of magic, an enchantment that has to do with time, which is always cross-pollinated between past and future: this is why each thing is not just an object unto itself, but in itself, in its irreducible uniqueness. No heterogeneous combinations here. Each room reflects a specific ethnicity, which finds its space not solely in the soul that sees it, but also on an imaginary geographic map that travels upon one's emotions. From Japan to Morocco, from Ethiopia to India with no need for a passport. Suffice it to open a door to change country and admire the paintings of the Australian artist Sidney Nolan in the long corridor used as a library, where a series of bookshelves behind grates display other treasures to be discovered. Or we can pause to look at the drawings by the Aboriginal artist Ngarra, the starting point of Alistair and Athena's last collection.

On the first floor, the thick stone walls and the vaulted ceiling create a cool, relaxing atmosphere even on the hottest summer days. The beds all differ, with high-quality linen sheets and lots of colorful pillows and blankets that add a touch of local warmth and tradition. Next to them carved wooden tables host a pitcher for water and an antique oil lamp whose light is soft and welcoming in the evening hours. The furniture is enriched by artisanal details: woven baskets that contain aromatic plants, a painting on ceramic by a local artist, and handwoven carpets that give the terracotta floors a touch of color and texture. The bathrooms are simple, featuring open showers and large stone bathtubs, underscoring just how little luxury has to do with wealth, but, rather, is at one with beauty. All we need to do is explore the gardens, or simply sit on the benches in the courtyard filled

with rare ferns, cacti, and succulents, and observe the swallows swooping down from the arches of the cloister to understand that a simple gesture is worth more than any luxury. The garden, where the pool almost seems to be a concession to the unbridled "opulence," is Athena's place, her daily delight and concern. At one time, this green realm was cared for by Alistair who, being a good Englishman, elevated gardening to a personal and cultural artform. Now it reflects the sensitivity and the touch of the lady of the house, who has downsized and renewed some of her husband's creations, while maintaining his vision unaltered. The challenges were considerable, climate change and Xylella, and required a fitting answer: sturdy and resistant plant life that needed less water so it would prosper in spite of the adversities. This adaptation created a symphony of plants that bloom year-round. In the garden, a colorful rug comes to life in spring, with over 100,000 bulbs of anemones, crocuses, tulips, and dwarf irises. May brings with it the glory of roses and bearded irises, as the wildflowers reach their own height of splendor. The summer, instead, is filled with the intense fragrance of the jasmines, lilies, agapanthuses, and the colors of the bougainvillea. Lastly, fall is the season for pomegranates and quinces, ready to be harvested. On the balconies, the succulents prosper stubbornly, in spite of the scorching heat and the lack of rain. In Salento water is a precious asset, so Athena has chosen to limit the amount of irrigation, preferring a watering can out of parsimony and respect. As Voltaire wrote: "One must cultivate one's own garden,"[3] not just with fertilizer and hoes, but above all with care. Of the kind one perceives in this Convent.

[1] Walter Benjamin, "Unpacking My Library," in *Selected Writings*, Vol. 2: 1931–1934 (Cambridge, MA, and London: Belknap Press, 2005), 487.
[2] Walter Benjamin, "Unpacking My Library."
[3] Voltaire, *Candide, or Optimism* (London: Penguin Classics, 2005), 124–125.

4.

The Convent garden offers several corners in which to linger and enjoy a meal outdoors, such as the large stone table, perfect for moments of conviviality. To the left, one of the flowered paths, the realm of lilies, agapanthuses, and bougainvillea.

4.

The long L-shaped corridor that separates the rooms becomes a rich catalog of collections filled with objects that tell stories of distant lands. To the right, the steps leading to the upper floor of the ancient cloister amid arches and star-shaped vaults.

Another living area, this one characterized by a crocodile hanging from the ceiling and an eclectic collection of objects and furnishings.
To the left, the cloister leads to a series of sitting rooms, such as this one with a fireplace, a cozy corner that unfolds around the old hearth.

The bathroom of one of the bedrooms on the upper floor,
with a bathtub set in the middle,
offers a uniquely relaxing experience.
To the right, one of the rooms on the ground floor, decorated by a four-poster bed
and details alluding to distant lands.

BAGNOLO DEL SALENTO

neverland

A radiant livery offset
by a cerulean brushstroke.
The hamlets of Salento,
all year-round, are flooded
by the daylight that seems to
infuse almost unreal purity
into every single thing.
The hours go by slowly,
accompanied by the droning
of the cicadas and the quiet
murmuring sound of the
people in the squares.

BAGNOLO DEL SALENTO

5. A VILLAGE HOME

THE MAJESTY OF WHITE, SIMPLE, AND SILENT

In this corner of the earth, the hectic rhythms of the modern world we are accustomed to seem distant. Quite the opposite of London, with its never-ending flow and crowded streets. Here, in the heel of the Italian peninsula, time is rarefied: there is no rush, no chaos, just the sweet melody of nature and the warmth of the community that in the morning might leave a basket filled with fruit outside your door. The slowness that in today's megalopolises is considered an obstacle in Bagnolo del Salento—a small town just a few miles from the more aristocratic Tricase and Maglie—becomes a precious resource. It is a world apart, where the soul finds shelter and one's heart is filled with peace. This is especially true for people like François Man, an interior designer from London, who had been searching for a corner of tranquility in which to seize the moment and turn it into an experience of emotional independence. Man was not looking for an all-inclusive, disposable holiday package, however. He did not want something immediate and superficial, because freedom is not a consumer good that you find on a supermarket shelf. It is a profound and vital need, something that is conquered one day at a time. A need that seven years ago for Man became a trip. Destination: Italy, the land of beauty without borders. And it was Puglia, and in particular Lower Salento—an island dressed up like a peninsula—which proved to be fatal for him. Here, in this corner of the world, the houses seem to be waiting patiently, ready to welcome anyone who is destined to be a part of them.

This is what also happened to Man, who, during one of his vacations headed out to Bagnolo to see that romantic and candid dwelling that had been waiting for him for some time. And now François, who in spite of his name is half Chinese and half German, when he is here, in this land he calls home, is simply known as Francesco. An Italian with the right to be one out of love and not because he was born here, as the Italian flag in his living room proudly informs us. A common infatuation around these parts. In the same way that everyone's feeling toward the homes in this area is a common one. No one ever disagrees: nothing is to be touched, everything (or almost everything) should be left the way it is.

It seems that these buildings so rich in history possess a sort of absolute inviolability inherent to their genetic makeup, and this appears to influence their new owners indistinctly. A "syndrome" that affected Man as well, in spite of the fact that he is accustomed by trade to work hard to give a new look to the homes of his clients with interventions that are much more radical. Although he is the director of Studio Reed, one of the most renowned in London, which works with a carefully selected clientele, the rules do not apply here. Tradition and history always win. This means that a heavy-handed renovation won't be necessary, a few jobs will suffice: the remodeling of the rooms on the top floor that at one time were home to rabbits and pigeons, that extra bathroom that has now become a necessity. The two outer staircases have also remained the same, and they are the only ones joining the two floors of the house. And little does it matter that the floors aren't perfectly even and the doors are small and low, all you need to do is bow your head slightly. The result of this is a familiar environment, far from the homogeneousness that threatens Puglia's architecture. For François, safeguarding historical houses and the architectural peculiarities of this quasi-island is an act of devotion toward a culture that risks dying out. Everything was already the way it should be, thanks also to the work that was done by the previous owner, a British artist who had moved to Bagnolo and lived there for a number of years. And before her, by another François, a French musician, who had already left his own light mark.

Signs of life that have never affected the spontaneous beauty of the house, with its candid, well-proportioned, but not necessarily symmetrical, surface: in this hamlet there is no room for urban clichés. White, enriched by blue details and capers growing on the roof—the plant resembles a rebellious tuft of hair, giving the building underneath a capricious air—the house reminds us of the beauty of Mediterranean homes. One might think it is just a stone's throw away from the sea, but it is actually around six miles by car. But the distance doesn't matter, because this land is almost an island in itself, squeezed between two seas. The wave moves in any case, and with it that feeling of an eternal holiday that one perceives as soon as they cross the threshold of a small wooden turquoise door. Inside, a warm and welcoming environment dedicated to conviviality reveals a strong identity that is unveiled in an articulated alcove, where elegant arches frame the dining room area. A table is at the center and around it are brickwork seats complete with striped cushions that decorate the space. This area is connected to the kitchen by a dumbwaiter set inside the wall. Next to the fireplace, featuring a mantelpiece in Leccese stone, is the area dedicated to preparing food. This space, which is characterized by its simplicity, is made of stone and curtained off at the bottom. The whole evokes tradition, but it gracefully avoids the risk of seeming overly rustic, thanks to the contemporary touch of the painting by the Australian artist Eduardo Santos above the stove. A quick glance is not enough to perceive the essence of the house. It is necessary to carefully explore what is on the walls, and to take a look at the *objets d'art* that François has chosen. This fusion of aesthetic visions creates a perfect balance between tradition and modernity, Salentine roots and global influences. Local touches, like the old pottery acquired by Rivesto, an antiques dealer in Lecce, and the artisanal weavings produced by Le Costantine, a workshop known for its collaboration with Maison Dior for the 2021 Cruise Collection, infuses authenticity and a deep connection with the region. The furnishings tell the story of a fascinating journey between eras and cultures, with each element selected to elicit stories and thoughts. Like the living room on the ground floor that astonishes for its simplicity. Very few carefully selected elements—a gray couch, a table whose top is an old carpenter's workbench, and two vintage Safari Chairs from the 1950s, at one time produced by Rud Rasmussen—create an atmosphere of sober elegance, in which each detail reflects authenticity and timeless taste. Next to the living room is the first bedroom, a discreet refuge framed by a stone vault that becomes one with the headboard, where each element seems to have been chosen to emphasize the naturalness of the environment, without needing to add anything else.

Outside, steps lead to the various terraces, corners protected from the summer heat that create an oasis of cool air, furnished with sofas and a perfect table for moments of tranquility. Above, the other bedrooms now welcome you with an essential and monastic style, allowing the structure of the house itself to tell its story. Once again, the interior design is filled with taste and parsimony: a double-door closet dating to the late eighteenth century and coming from the Luca di Gioia gallery in Maglie, a rattan armchair produced between the 1950s

3

A view of the dining area, with the Chatwin armchair by Richard Wrightman in the foreground. To the left, one of the outside corners sheltered from the summer heat that is transformed here into a cool oasis. The armchair is from the 1950s.

and 1960s by the German company Arco Schutzmarke, and rugs by the textile designer Christine Van Der Hurd add a touch of international elegance to the local warmth. Everything achieves a perfect balance between contemporary sensitivity and emotional depth, a romantic equation like the house, far from having the effect of a postcard or glossy magazine. The bathroom as well, respectfully renewed, reflects this philosophy: simplicity is the first word that comes to mind, but with a modern touch: a deep concrete bathtub that offsets this timeless context. Throbbing and vital, like the sentiments and the passions that inhabit it: that is how Man shaped it, so that it would be able to welcome small moments and shared rituals, becoming an intimate, dynamic, and all-encompassing setting for everyday life. No longer an explosion of indistinct stimuli, a frenetic flowing of everyday actions, but rather an epiphany: a gash in the sky, a vision that helps you to understand how you are fully present in the moment. The house then becomes a sort of island, where the limits between the past and the present, the outside world and domestic intimacy are dissolved in an eternal embrace.

This dwelling, like Salento itself, is a place suspended between eras and influences, a land that welcomes with the same generosity thousands of years of history and modern visions as well. Each detail of the house is an actor in this intimate setting, where the everyday becomes poetry, where every gesture–preparing a meal to welcome a guest–is a celebration of life. That is where the beauty lies, in the ability to transform the ordinary into the extraordinary, to make it so that each day, in this dwelling, becomes a ritual of reconciliation between the self and the world. This new experience no longer has cardinal points, because in this corner of the Mediterranean the journey is not so much a journey toward a physical place but toward a dimension of the soul. From whatever perspective we choose to look at this enticing landscape, it will always be endless. Just like an island.

On the previous page, under the star-shaped vaults of the ceilings, the masonry kitchen, whose lower portion is closed off by simple curtains.
Above, on the wall, some of the works of Andrea Collesano, whose art is inspired by nature, particularly the animal world.

A detail of the door, with a jar bought in an antiques market.
To the left, on the ground floor, the simplicity overwhelms you: a gray sofa,
a table made from an old carpenter's bench, and two Safari Chairs from the 1950s.

5.

5.

On the previous pages, two images describe precious details: a view that opens onto the roofs of the Salentine village and an outer staircase, simple and silent, that delicately extends upwards.

Below, two views of the bathroom, where simplicity is the byword, but with a modern touch that makes it unique: a concrete tub featuring an essential design, in contrast with everything around it, accentuating the feeling of coziness permeating the space.

To the right, located next to the living room is the first bedroom, a discreet and welcoming refuge, framed by a stone vault that seems to embrace the entire space here, blending in harmoniously with the headboard on the bed, creating visual continuity.

The bedroom on the upper floor features a double-door closet from the Luca di Gioia gallery in Maglie and a rattan chair made between the 1950s and '60s by the German company Arco Schutzmarke. To the right, a view of the almost monastic-style bedroom.

5.

SPONGANO

the house of drawings

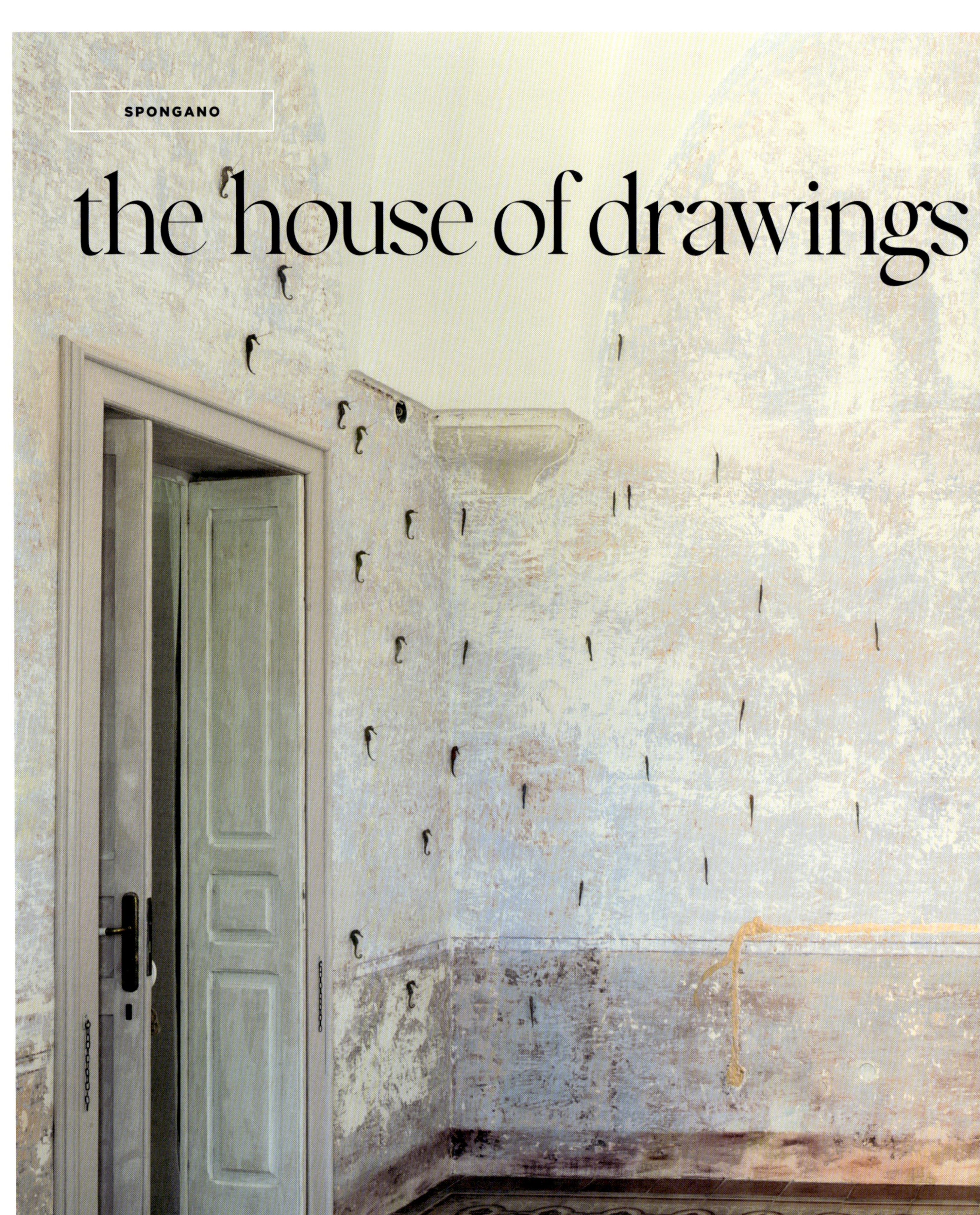

A fluttering of the eyelids.
Outside, the relentless
sunlight floods the
landscape with blinding
rays, so intense there
is a wildness about them.
Inside, the light softens,
filtering in through
the thick, light-hued
walls of the house.

SPONGANO

6. A VILLAGE DWELLING
LINES THAT
TELL STORIES

At last, the gaze rests for a moment, like in church when the eye becomes accustomed to the cool, suffuse light of a holy space. It takes a few seconds to get used to it. But in no time at all, suddenly you are enveloped by a profound, luminous candor, filled with light and shadow. The peaceful atmosphere in this house instantly reveals its secret: it is the home of two creatives, where everything speaks of art, but it is also a refuge for the family that tells a story about their love and passion for Puglia.

Discovered when it was in a dilapidated state, this centuries-old construction in the heart of Spongano, in the province of Lecce, a small village just four miles from the sea, was completely remodeled with such care and respect that it still preserves traces of its past. The building, with its thick walls made of Lecce stone, the calcareous rock typical of the area, features an articulated plan that still tells of how the village life that unfolded inside those imposing walls must have been. Though not an aristocratic *magione*, it is still steeped in memories and tales, which, thanks to the owners who restructured it respectfully, has turned into a new chapter to be written and drawn in new colors. All these stories are right there, close at hand, as one focuses on the grit floor surmounted by star-shaped vaults following each other between the kitchen and the large living room, or discovers an old piece of pottery tucked inside a niche in the wall, the memory of bygone times. The owners, Luciana Di Virgilio and Gianni Veneziano, who in their trade go by the name of Di Virgilio Veneziano—a couple originally from Puglia, who arrived in Milan, the promised land for all those who make creativity their trade—spend the summers here in the company of Virginia, their young daughter, because here alone can their dreams come true. Luciana, a designer filled with curiosity and dynamism, is an explorer constantly searching for new forms of expression. Gianni, an artist devoted to design, knows the secret of how to transform the everyday into poetry. These are the gifts they have passed on to the youngest in the family, who, paintbrush in hand, never shrinks from following her father around as he adds painted images around the house. Such as those for the new winding staircase, made of brutalist concrete, that, in the midst of wall paintings depicting vases and birds, leads to the roof terrace. Signs and drawings that quickly reveal another key to interpretation: the characterizing of a component with a graphic element, be it a hand-painted tile, or an imperfection, like a crack in the wall, that comes back to life thanks to gilding, offering a new identity to a surface that was once white, or a tower with a staircase that wasn't there before.

This is exactly the direction chosen to enhance the typical aspects of the place, such as the vaults and the original wall decorations hidden beneath layers of paint, as well as the finishings in cement tiles and the flooring in Lecce stone. It is a decision based on the acceptance of the passing of time as an integral part of life and of art. As with *wabi-sabi*, the Japanese aesthetic that peacefully welcomes the fleetingness and imperfection of things, here, too, time feels as if suspended. New finishings, like the *tadelakt*—an ancient Moroccan technique that involves the use of a highly resistant plaster to create a surface pleasing to the touch—adopted here for the bathrooms and kitchen, harmonize with the pre-existing ones, the result of which is a symphonic effect that never seems out of place.

Thanks to the work that was done, the circulation flows better: an internal concrete spiral staircase and the opening of new windows made it possible to open up the dwelling to the air and the light, thus allowing the wind that changes with the seasons to blow through the old walls. A beauty rediscovered, where the decoration, that is barely whispered, expresses obligatory poetry where even a shadow, a crack in the wall, reveals a secret power. "There is a crack, a crack in everything, that's how the light gets in," sang Leonard Cohen in his husky voice in *Anthem*. And that is how an electrical tracing on the wall in Virginia's room, once a flaw to be eliminated, is now a work of art thanks to the gilding carried out by father and daughter together. With surprising results, because, as *kintsugi*, the ancient Japanese art of repairing ceramics with gold teaches us, cracks can generate rebirth. Ask the dust–to borrow the title of John Fante's novel–to understand that here the emotion that travels along the thread of memory is fed by imperfections, and moves like a cold north wind that shakes the leaves of thousand-year-old olive trees, unyielding witnesses to the passing of time.

Outside, on the facade, the aqua green chosen for the walls seems to bestow continuity and even some courage upon the Mediterranean plant life, which is sometimes at the mercy of the hot sun. The tower enclosing the staircase, illuminated by small arched windows, rises up to the sky like a village watchtower without pretending to have a military function, while a long and narrow swimming pool surrounded by greenery becomes a cool haven on the hottest days of summer. From the tallest point of the tower, Paola Citterio, an artist with Milanese roots and a New York soul, has woven the air with the work *ho colorato lu jentu*, hand-knitted with merino wool. Not simply a tapestry, but the site-specific fusion between place and media, conceived to embrace the house like a secret whispered by the breeze.

In the garden, an irregularly shaped table becomes an installation recalling a mother's womb, a refuge that incorporates the tree, the expression of the ethical-aesthetic concept of recycling what has been discarded, something that is so dear to this couple. Produced with artisanal know-how by Mondial Marmi, this one-off piece becomes a sentimental collage, where the recycled stones tell stories of respect and sensitivity. Once again, Gianni makes a drawing on the tabletop, impressing a sign enhancing the silent voice of the place, transforming it into a symbol of memory and poetry.

The ground floor, which is directly connected to the outdoors, consists of a large living room and a kitchen with dining area. At the center of the living room, the carpet created by the couple for the *Parola* collection, by Carpet Edition, unfolds like a silent letter addressed to those who travel here. It is truly a vehicle of meanings, hand-painted, that converses with the period fabrics covering the sofas, found in the markets, woven on a loom, designed by the owner of the house, and then sewn by an embroiderer from Spongano. Symbols that unwind between nature and faces, telling stories suspended between past and present. The brickwork structure finished in plaster is a suite of star-shaped vaults, underscored by solid ribbing that is strong enough to uphold the ancient construction. The decor is an exquisite array of objects that includes ancient ceramics, family souvenirs, the icons of the history of design, pieces designed by the couple, antique furnishings purchased from Luca di Gioia of Maglie, and artistic installations. All it takes are two stones and a recycled wooden plank to create a bench. Basic, true, but with an artwork above it everything changes.

63
65

4

In the kitchen area, the large island is one of Gianni's creations. The owner of the house has etched by hand around five hundred tiles created by Giuseppe Colì (master potter and world lathe champion) of Fratelli Colì. This local craftsmanship produces works in clay shaped perfectly according to the teachings handed down from one generation to the next. The dining room area next to the large windows overlooking the garden features a simple decor. A bench made of stone recycled from the old staircase and a niche in the thick wall made as per tradition in Lecce stone, complete the scene, so ethereal and white it is almost monastic. Some of the walls, and many of the doors, have maintained the brushwork of the past and the signs of the time, remaining in keeping with a tale that is constantly changing, in which overlapping traces intertwine, and through a game of colors, scratches, and flaws reveal a visual and tactile depth that would otherwise be impossible.

A pointed arch, among the many that define the spaces here, shows the way to the concrete winding staircase that leads toward the bedrooms, where Gianni's studio becomes a delicate screen between the world of sleep and that of creativity. Beneath the ceiling, the atmosphere is tinged with imperceptibly fading hues from green to pink, from blue to yellow. The path, closed off by white curtains, once again becomes an artistic installation, a room within a room, so light as to never even touch the ceiling. The bedroom of the youngest of the family, where the electrical tracing on the wall has been repaired with gilded additions, is decorated with only a few pieces of furniture, all of which are capable of telling a story, like the famous chair by Charles and Ray Eames, now manufactured by Vitra, found abandoned on the street and given a new life with painting and decorative carving. The cabinets, custom-made to a design by the owners, are the work of a Pugliese artisan, the idea being to highlight local production. A tangible sign of just how important the region and its remarkable skilled workers are for Luciana and Gianni. Lastly, the master bedroom, which features a green bathroom made using recycled materials, such as the column washbasin from the 1970s, found abandoned with other building materials in a local market, is replete with designer pieces. Much like the house as a whole, filled with the couple's art collection, which includes the installation *Unicorn* by the artist Antonio Fiorentino, previously exhibited in New York, pieces by Yuval Avital, Marta Baldo, Pasquale Gadaleta, Fathi Hassan, Giuseppe Maraniello, and Gianni Veneziano, the protagonist and curator of international shows, who donated to the Triennale di Milano the *Fondo Gianni Veneziano – Il segno dei designer*. A blend of art and tradition, design and anonymous pieces that have not simply emerged from the factory, aiming to underscore the extent to which this house is a constantly evolving life project, focused on its existential use by the owners, nomads by nature. A different idea that transformed this home into a unique place and that, through a special blend of activities—art gallery, guest house, and venue in which to hold events—is constantly transformed and adapted to different functions. A space in which to vacation, a place of exchange and work, a cultural and artistic center where the lines between private and public are blurred, interweaving in a harmony of fluidity that only architecture, design, and art can make possible. A project that is open every day to new possibilities and new designs, to new colors. After all, you cannot stop the wind, and when it comes it carries new dreams with it.

MANGIA

DISEGNA

IL FUTURO DEI MUSEI È NELLE NOSTRE CASE

6.

On the previous pages, in the midst of the star-shaped vaults in the living room, a few carefully selected pieces: two roughly hewn stones and a recycled wooden table come together to breathe life into a minimalist bench filled with memories. Above, a detail of the cement-tiled floor that recalls traditional artisanship, and of the sofa, finished with a fabric embroidered following a pattern by Gianni Veneziano. To the right, the new concrete staircase, simply designed and embellished with a wall painting by the owner.

6.

In the bathroom with the tadelakt tub, a 1970s washbasin by Catalano and a mirror, both of which were found in an antiques market.

To the right, the suite is adorned with the Pelota lamp by Ponzio and Casati for Lamperti. Hanging on the wall is the work La nascita di Spina *by Pasquale Gadaleta.*

On the following pages, the bedroom of the daughter of the family is furnished with very few items, all of them capable of telling a story, like the two specially designed cabinets made by a local artisan and a painting by the young artist Marta Baldo.

ORGOGLIO
PREGIUDIZIO

sunday lunch

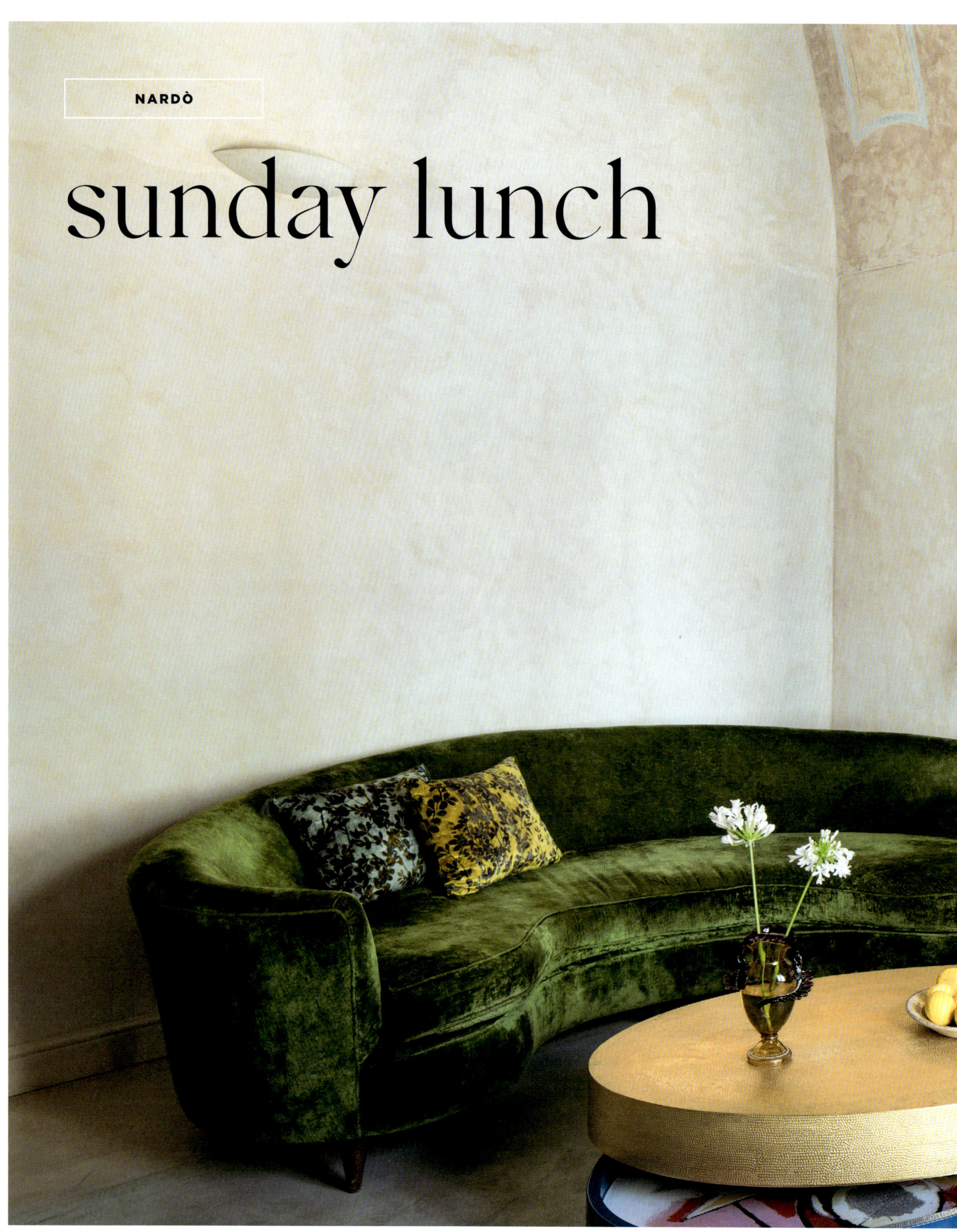

In summer, the days seem
to awaken only at sunset,
just when the sun decides
to lower its gaze and the light
wearily surrenders.
It is at that moment that the
stone, saturated with heat,
seems to breathe, like a heart
finally easing its weight.

NARDÒ

7. PALAZZO MUCI
WHERE HOSPITALITY REIGNS SUPREME

Shadows and the last rays of light chase one another along the facades and arches, caressing every corner with a brush soaked in gold. We are in Nardò, a jewel of Baroque architecture also known as the "little Lecce," situated just a twenty-minute drive from the natural wonders of the Porto Selvaggio Park and the Palude del Capitano. A town—the second largest in Salento—that still today tells its noble story through swirls of garlands, cherubs, and figures reminiscent of characters painted by Bosch, as if it were an open book in a symphonic crescendo of columns, loggias, and capitals. A haven of urban elegance gathered around the sixteenth-century Acquaviva Castle, with its ancient moat filled in and converted into a garden, and Piazza Salandra, a stage of theatrical beauty crowned by the spire of the Immaculate Conception, rising up among churches and noble palaces.

Nardò does not hide and cannot be passed by unnoticed: its bold beauty emerges through alleys steeped in history, asserting itself naturally, stone by stone. Here, the past slips through one's fingers like fine sand, leaving an imperceptible yet indelible mark on those who gaze upon it. It does not need to boast to capture attention. Its strength lies in its authenticity, capable of surprising even those accustomed to the dazzling pace of metropolises like Paris. Such was the case for the renowned Michelin-starred chef Guy Martin, who, while on vacation with his family in 2015, was enchanted by the charm of this location—a sweet and unexpected trap that seduced him with its Baroque curls and has not let him go since then. He too was swept away by that strange alchemy that has drawn many seemingly distant lives to this land, which, step by step, as if guided by an invisible hand, found themselves meeting here. And without any forewarning or plan, not even for someone like Guy—a wanderer of myriad stories, cultures, and passions, always one step beyond the ordinary—who over the years has collected Michelin stars, cookbooks, TV appearances, and restaurants from Switzerland to France, and from China to Polynesia, was it possible to resist the allure of this timeless landscape of shifting light tones. Despite his global adventures, here in this land where time follows only the heartstrings, his gaze was softened, becoming a reflection of the soul.

At first, the dream was a simple one: to buy a house where he could host his friends during vacations. But he got carried away: an ancient residence, then another, and yet another. Today, Palazzo Muci, Maritati, and Matteo—his special three "M"s (coincidentally matching the first letter of his last name)—stand as three intimate and refined eighteenth-century guest houses, located a short distance from one another and from Piazza Salandra. Close yet distinct, each holds stories of families and lives to tell, with small courtyards, secret gardens, and terraces overlooking the white alleyways that have brought worldwide fame to Salento. Years of meticulous workmanship were needed to restore the beauty of these spaces, largely thanks to Guy's wife, Katherina Marx, an interior designer. With the help of Jérôme Faillant-Dumas, former artistic director for Yves Saint Laurent and Dior, and her fine taste, she connected the ancient stones with modernity.

Here, in the remote corners of southern Italy, bathed in sunlight, wind, and a timeless gentle light,

Guy Martin welcomes his guests into spaces where culture and landscape merge. These places embody a fusion of identity, history, and contemporary art. Visitors are greeted in rooms blending Eastern influences with echoes of music, art, and literature, all immersed in natural light and the allure of the local stone. Every detail, carefully chosen by Katherina, the project's artistic director, converses with the spirit of the place, transforming each sojourn into a journey through art and history. The result: three unexpected gems, all waiting to be discovered.

First among them is Palazzo Muci, with its entrance framed by dazzlingly white columns, supporting a semicircular archway closed off by a wrought-iron gate. Stepping through the threshold, it takes just a moment for the light to explode, flooding the space: a white courtyard, like a pause in the silence, opens onto the garden, where every shadow fades, and the whiteness reflects the serenity of this timeless place. A brightness that is almost blinding yet softens inside, where with its immaculate livery it seems to caress every surface. It is a setting that makes the invisible visible, the immaterial tangible, and enhances the magic of the place. Credit goes to the careful restoration carried out by architects Luigi and Sabina Ripa and Giancarlo De Pascalis, who succeeded in preserving the *magione*'s architectural essence. After all, in Salento walls are not demolished; they are preserved, delicately repainted, and, if traces of the past survive, they are lovingly safeguarded.

On the ground floor, the rooms follow one from the other, separated by large arches beneath tall ceilings, which still bear the traces of ancient frescoes. The pearly floors, like the vaulted ceilings, are gentle on the eyes, cradling the gaze with a creamy softness that embraces the space without dominating it. Some arches, with their Moorish lines, tell the stories of people who came by sea, as this land has always welcomed those desiring to stay. A subtle language flows through the house, where every corner, understated and discreet, is furnished with the thoughtful eye of someone from afar, yet it never betrays the soul of the stone, which here remains the true master. Every piece of art, every book, every design object is a memory, a fragment of history, drawn from the collection of Guy—the Michelin-starred chef of Paris's historic Le Grand Véfour—and his wife, Katherina.

Spread harmoniously over three floors, Palazzo Muci is a fusion of art and history, the result of delicate eclecticism that blends furnishings with painstaking care. Take the vintage green velvet sofa and the oval table designed by Davide Caprioli, an architect at Pomellato and a friend of the owner, skillfully paired with Gio Ponti's 1950s Ninfea armchair and Tommaso Barbi's Ginkgo lamp from the 1970s. A sophisticated touch of gold embellishes the wardrobe, as if to affirm that a hint of glamour is always welcome, even here, among the stones of Italy's heel. In the dining room, a set of vintage wicker chairs encircles a late-nineteenth-century table, while on the wall, *Opera Visiva* paintings by Claudine Drai tell of a fragile world animated by ephemeral paper figures.

The bedrooms are a fascinating anthology of contrasts, as in the Superior Suite Colomba on the first floor, where Alvar Aalto chairs, symbols of

clean Scandinavian lines and function, are joined by Tapio Wirkkala's table and Aino Aalto's chandelier. These blend seamlessly with a collection of African statues and a Caravane sofa, whose stacked mattresses evoke an Eastern atmosphere. Or in the Arcangela room, a veritable tribute to design: from Gaetano Pesce's Spaghetti vase for Fish Design, to Ettore Sottsass's Pausania lamp, still being produced by Artemide. These elements engage masterfully with the lighting by Enza Fasano, a ceramic artist from Grottaglie, and with artistic accents from François Dautresme's Chinese textiles collection, cleverly highlighted by Katherina. Then there's the Olivia Suite, adorned with delicate Tissus Chinois fabrics and bamboo furniture, brought to life by a vibrant painting in the sitting area, a *Tableau Cercles* by Geneviève Claisse, the French abstract artist who sculpted geometric precision into her intense and vivid canvases.

The designer pieces include Ico Parisi's bookshelf and a work by Torrick Ablack, better known as Toxic, one of the early street artists. Both find a home in the Ippazia Suite, where classical charm intertwines with contemporary creative rebellion, generating an unexpected dialogue that lends balance and character to the space. Every part of the house lives and breathes in perfect harmony with the outdoor spaces, thanks to two terraces offering enchanting views of nearby palace profiles and an L-shaped pool, nestled geometrically in the lush garden. Here, the intense sunlight dances with the greenery, creating shimmering reflections on the water's surface. A striking colonnade embraces this Mediterranean oasis, where mandarin trees, jasmine, and abundant agapanthus flowers seem to compete as if in a beauty pageant.

But this is not the only residence. A short walk away reveals another arched portal, supported by columns, which guards another treasure: Palazzo Matteo. Here, amid colorful vaulted ceilings and lush palm trees, rests a vintage Fiat 500 Topolino, witness to an Italy that once dreamed and raced toward modernity. Furniture, books, and vintage objects intertwine in this home's design narrative: from Marcel Breuer's leather TECTA-D4 (B4) chairs to Ettore Sottsass's Beverly sideboard for Memphis, and the Curvadio cabinet, a unique piece by Luigi Serafini. A visual journey blending memory and creativity, telling a story where every detail echoes the past while looking toward the future.

Lastly, one more gem: Palazzo Maritati, the most "French" of the three. Like its counterparts, it gathers Guy and Katherina's world into a sophisticated universe that reveals its essence in the simplicity of what truly matters. Genuine, honest, and capable of warming the heart with just a few natural ingredients, like a family meal.

These three homes pay tribute to Salento. Here, the spirit of business is irrelevant; only the beauty of a people who know how to share everything, like being at the table together, really matters. Time here seems to slow down as if it were The Seventh Day, a Sunday, because in Salento, time isn't measured: it's experienced.

The famous chef's collection of ancient ceramics.
To the left, the dining room with a series of vintage wicker chairs around a late-nineteenth-century table.
Two artworks titled Opera Visiva *by Claudine Drai hang on the walls.*

7.

7.

A detail of the Ippazia room, with Ico Paris bookshelves, Le Corbusier's Parliament lamp, and, to the right, one of the bathrooms in the suites.

To the right, the Arcangela room, with Chinese textiles on the wall from the François Dautresme collection, cleverly displayed by Katherina Marx.

The very high ceilings in the Superior Suite Colomba, with star-shaped vaults, and a terrace on the upper floor, express timeless elegance. To the right, in the suite's sitting room, Alvar Aalto's Le Fauteuils chairs are perfectly matched with the sculptural table by Tapio Wirkkala.

PETER LINDBERGH

the tower's winning move

Every place brings with
it a memory that, like
the wind, at times caresses
the countryside, shaping
the landscape, and
at other times stops
and remains motionless.
Imprinted on the walls
of the *masserie*, ancient
parchments harbor the
deeds of a past that has
never stopped fighting.

SALVE

8. MASSERIA PALACI

A CHESSBOARD SURROUNDED BY OLIVE TREES

These are stone skeletons, the silent witnesses of many generations that have dedicated themselves with archaic devotion to the land, akin to the way you caress a face that may be weary but is still dear to you. Here, the events were not handed down only by way of volumes of history but mostly thanks to the eloquent silences of objects. They know truths that escape us, and, if they find a clever interpreter, they can recount stories that have been forgotten, and add others as well. After all, the material of those walls is like an impression made in fresh clay: it preserves every groove and crack traced by the passage of time, a memory shaped by the hand of man and the slow erosion of the elements, but never entirely erased. Only transformed. All that is required is a trace of the past, like a small, ancient fifteenth-century tower that turns pink when the sun sets, so that the story can start over again. That is what happened in the countryside around Salve—a few miles from Marina di Pescoluse, a sun-kissed paradise that tourists call the "Maldives of Salento"—where the only intact survivor of a large rural complex remained perched on itself for a long time, like a sentinel amid ruins waiting to be rediscovered.

It was neither an "ivory tower," nor a symbol of nobility; it was, and still is, a sign of a farmer's pride, in a land of sharecroppers, proud in its rustic simplicity. And it is precisely this austere, almost brutalist aspect that bewitched Francesco Russo, an eclectic designer and a visionary, born right in the heel of Italy, who began his career as a shoe designer, collaborating with various brands like Costume National, Miu Miu, Yves Saint Laurent, Dior. Lots of experiences with some of the greatest names, and then his own steps, with his own brand. Restless and indomitable—like his wild horses, when they were still untamed—he studied in Milan, followed by a long period in Paris and in Switzerland, before returning to the capital of the Lombard region and to his native land. Always with a plane ticket in his pocket, between one trip and another, one day he visited a friend in Bari. A magazine leafed through by chance at the airport, and the idea of the *masseria* instantly became a desire for discovery. For some time he had been looking for a place to go to on vacation, and, in the end, he was love-struck by the tower surrounded by ruins that would soon become the Masseria Palaci.

A trail, a few dry walls that still bordered the farmyard, and around it an expanse of fertile hills, where the once luxuriant olive trees made their leaves glisten in the sun, and the water of the Canale dei Fani—not too far away—flowed smoothly along a reed bed. Acquired in 2008, the *magione* was in a state of complete abandonment, and even the small bulwark made of tuff, albeit intact, still required consolidation.

For Francesco, restoration of the complex, which began in 2009, was a complicated and laborious task. It required working "a secco," the way the ancients had, to treat the wounds caused by neglect and time. Driven by tradition, the result is an architecture that seems, both inside and outside, almost spartan, so as to avoid ever interrupting the dialogue with the landscape and deceiving history. Francesco's touch is a delicate one, like that of the person who walks through the past on tiptoe, leaving signs that are never too deep. The ancient L-shaped building, lovingly rebuilt in its missing parts, seems embraced by a stone wall that, in the manner of a silent guardian, has always safeguarded the boundaries of a distant time.

The swimming pool, deliberately off to one side and parallel to the main courtyard, blends with the karstic depression that laps the estate. A circle of fertile land—

enclosed and protected by a rustic wall, which welcomes the slight slope in the level of the land and shields the citrus trees from the wind—reflects that ancient wisdom that knows how to follow the seasons and understand the earth. Francesco, like a skilled landscapist, has followed the land and shaped the undulations between the pool and the natural basin with large concrete steps finished with *cocciopesto* (fragments of earthenware). Minimal and brutalist in their simplicity, these were transformed by adding cushions into a large seating area, under the shade of a bamboo shelter. The steps, which appear to emerge from the ground itself, thus provide comfortable seats from which to contemplate the reflection of the water, in perfect continuity with the landscape.

On the opposite side of the ancient courtyard, Francesco has built two new buildings: one for the custodian's family, and the other dedicated to the gym, both connected to the main body by a Renaissance-style colonnade enveloped by a climbing vine. But the real heart of this tale is the tower and the L-shaped building, where it all began, with its four grassy quadrants where conversations interweave together and dinner is served outside, protected by an iron and river-cane roof. Along the facade, the promise of shade invites one to relax amid natural wood decor, almost primitive in its effective essentiality.

The kitchen, which was too small, was enlarged with a veranda overlooking the courtyard, serving as a connection for the staircase leading to the tower; before it could only be reached via an outer ramp. On one side, there is an operative space with a central counter; on the other, a corner opens up that merges gently between inside and outside, characterized by large windows that can be opened. The effect provides light and goes perfectly with the opaque and contemporary *cocciopesto* surfaces. These are interwoven harmoniously with a shelf made from simple wooden planks, creating a symbolic bridge between past and present.

Throughout the house this dialogue between eras is reflected in the use of traditional materials, walls finished in plaster and floors paved with natural soil, which fit in perfectly with the elements of modern antiques. A light osmosis links each thing like a slender aesthetic wire joining the icons of twentieth-century design, handmade objects found in the markets, and decor created specially by Francesco with recycled material. All in harmony, like the large fireplace, the protagonist of the daytime space, which matches to perfection the two armchairs and the Ragno table, signed by Carlo De Carli. On the walls there are very few elements: just two paintings by the contemporary artist Aaron Young add a touch of color, while the hanging lamps Viscontea and Taraxacum Cocoon, designed by the Castiglioni brothers and still produced today by Flos, sway lightly in the air.

The dining area as well expresses a sober elegance, devoid of ostentation: a large, solid wood table, simple and robust, of the kind used in a Franciscan dining hall, surrounded by 1950s chairs, purchased at an antiques market, and in the background two closets made with the shutters of old doors. A side door delicately opens onto a long hallway: here the bedrooms follow one another like pearls strung with an invisible thread. Wrapped in a peaceful atmosphere, the rooms have walls that are bare but warm, framed by a series of vaults; all frills are banished, except for the odd detail in style, like the lights, and a few erudite references, like Franco Albini's Margherita sofa, still produced by Bonacina.

At the end of the long hallway, like some unexpected surprise, a door opens onto the area of the pool, offering a view of what is truly a corner of paradise. Here the water reflects the sky, an oasis of peace and cool where every detail seems to be designed to celebrate beauty in its purest form, a perfect combination of nature, design, and architecture. Masseria Palaci is also a guest house with the plain common sense of rural architecture, but mediated by Francesco's cultured aesthetic vision, that of someone who has interpreted ancient tales while respecting local traditions, bringing them back to the present time. Starting from the tower, which continues to observe from above and dominates the scene still today. That is where everything began, and it is also where everything has returned. That small and austere sentinel, the bulwark of the land and of its people toiling in the fields, has regained its role, no longer as a guardian against faraway invaders, but as the ambassador of a new life. Its deep-rooted and solid presence is what marks the slow and solemn rhythm of the *masseria*, like a blistering move in a game of chess. With its motionless and still gaze, it observes the changing of the seasons and listens to the wind, silent yet vigilant, the participant in a story that has never stopped being transformed, just like the stones that have learned to survive. It is the victory of a remote and distant place that continues to be reborn, despite the difficulties, keeping alive the memory of what was and what will always be. It is a victory for Francesco, too, who has chosen this land because of his deep respect for nature, great passion for the animals and the people who live here, who have turned hospitality into a lesson so precious it is handed down from generation to generation. And so, as the glow of the sunset wraps itself around the *masseria*, the tower turns pink again and looks down from its humble pulpit. Witness to a land that, like its inhabitants, is capable of welcoming and giving.

*A detail of the traditional dry walls.
To the left, the swimming pool, which is deliberately detached from the structure, unfolds in parallel with the main courtyard, blending with the karstic depression that laps a part of the estate.*

Another point of view over the long and narrow swimming pool.
To the right, the colonnade wrapped in climbing vines that connects the old building to one of the two new blocks, one for the custodian, the other for a gym.

Aceto
Olio

One of the bathrooms of the rooms on the ground floor of the old building.
To the right, a detail of the room with a small masonry staircase, no longer in use,
which becomes an ornamental element amid the lime-finished vaults.

8.

BASSOTTO

DEPRESSA

by dint of being wind

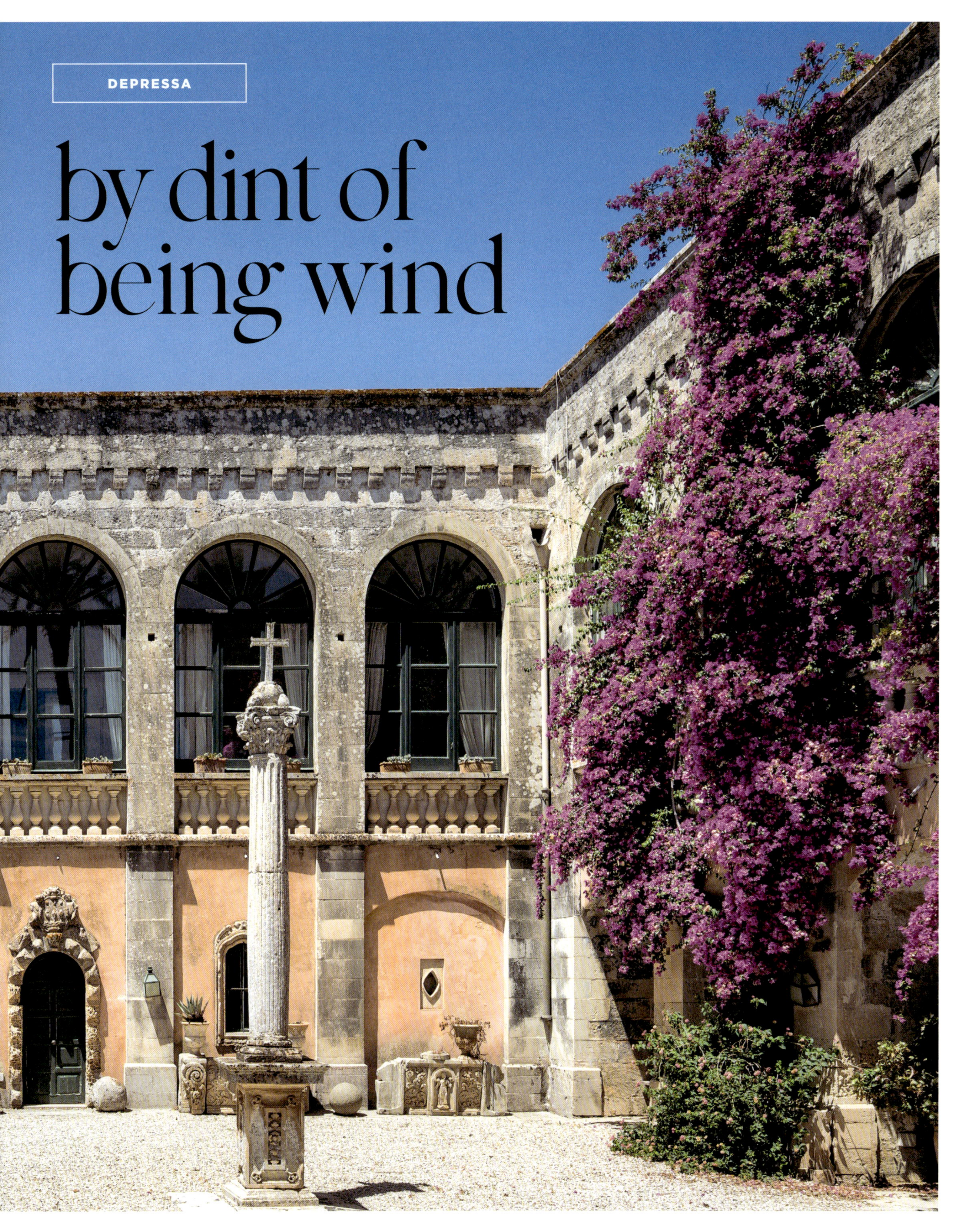

Everything seems to be
motionless here, but it's not.
It's just a deception.
Salento, as Carmelo Bene—
who was born in this very
province—wrote, is a "nomadic
land that revolves on itself."
It is a vortex of wind that gathers
and hands down stories,
from one generation to the next;
it is the sting of the tarantula
that exorcises one's inner
demons in order to celebrate
life instead.

9. CASTLE
BACKDROPS CONCEALING ANCIENT BATTLEMENTS

Here we are in Depressa, a small suburb of Tricase, thirty miles from Lecce and just four from the sea, a place that, under the somber irony of its name, hides a noble history that over the centuries has brought together the cultures of many countries. Here, the walls of Winspeare Castle and its austere Angevin tower, erected in the fourteenth century, are the witnesses to a rich and complex past, consisting of nobiliary life interwoven with the rural world. All one from an architectural point of view as well, seeing that the fortification built with engraved stone is part and parcel of this small town. Currently, the property belongs to Francesco Winspeare, a winemaker, and his brother Edoardo, a cult film director, descendants of the noble Anglo-Neapolitan family. It is here, where everything ends and everything appears to be on the verge of beginning again, that for generations they have laid their roots. Two cosmopolitans with lots of passports, who speak multiple languages—including the Salentine dialect—and who have never turned their blue-bloodedness into something to flaunt. Actually, they play around and joke about it with a touch of irony, seeing that, in response to the family coat of arms—"Depressus non victus" (Depressed, but not defeated)—they have offered another epigraph: "Roma caput mundi, sed Depressa secundi" (Rome is the first capital of the world, but Depressa comes second). Clearly a reflection of their love for this Salentine hamlet, as well as their hardly concealed humor toward the rhetoric of aristocracy. Umberto Eco wrote, in the finale of his novel *The Name of the Rose*, "Nomina nuda tenemus" (Names are all we have), to emphasize that names are just conventions. And so Depressa can change its name and become "Disperata" in Edoardo Winspeare's film *La vita in comune* (2017). But even with another equally inauspicious synonym, in that small godforsaken town in the South, one can still learn to dream. And you dream when you enter the castle, which in its long history has gone through a lot, including the Turkish invasion of 1480. And after that, the reconstructions, the demotion to farmstead, property transactions, and marriages, until the decisive one, in 1883, between Emanuela Gallone, daughter of the seventh Prince of Tricase, and Antonio Winspeare, Duke of Salve. The date marked the renewal of the structure and the beginning of a new chapter in the history of the English household of Catholic faith, which settled in the Italian peninsula as early as 1708, following the wars of religion in the British islands.

In the refurbishment of the castle, which it would appear was commissioned from the architect Filippo Bacile di Castiglione, the Duke preserved the sixteenth-century's quadrangular plan with two square towers, the loggiato (closed in the nineteenth century), the monumental staircase, the machicolation at the main entrance, and, on the western side, the platforms supporting the wall walk. He also finished enlarging the rectangular courtyard, adding a terrace with a portico, and he built a home for the keeper's family. His great-grandson Riccardo Winspeare later completed the refurbishment by building a small loggia, a kitchen, and a supplementary staircase overlooking the secondary courtyard, thus bestowing on the estate its definitive form. A long and labored history that feels like a film plot. Just as in Edoardo's films—he is the cantor of this corner of the region, whose "accidental actors" recite their parts in dialect—who in his most recent work, *Vita mia*, allows everyone to enter the castle together with Dominique Sanda, a noblewoman inspired by the filmmaker's mother, accompanied by a Salentine assistant. It is an impassioned tale

of Europe and World War Two seen through the lens of the very close friendship between two completely different women, who, as they move about in their resigned serenity, between Transylvania and Depressa, rediscover themselves in spite of their social differences. Or perhaps they reacquire the past precisely because of this diversity, for in this ancient fief on the edge of this unknown region, any disparities in rank seem to have been swept away by time, as if kidnapped by the incessant wind swirling around them. In Salento, the social status of the person who tilled the soil was less dramatic with respect to other Southern Italian regions, thanks to the small land ownership that defused tensions. The locals here, who at one time viewed even the citizens of the nearby towns as "furastieri" (foreigners) and even went so far as to call anyone who came from beyond the border "svizzeri" (Swiss), continue to welcome people arriving from elsewhere with the same discreet spontaneity with which, in the last century, they opened the castle doors for Princess Margaret of England. Time here is more than a mere concept: it is culture and lifeblood. The thread of history has handed down obsessions, verses, and nostalgia, like the ones that we read in between the battlements of this castle.

The entrance to the castle, situated in a small square, is austere and preserves the beauty of the past as if it wanted to be reassuring thanks to its majestic familiarity, but without any surprises. The side facade, devoid of excessive vertical thrusts, fits in harmoniously with the surrounding houses, without ever competing with their height. Nonetheless, the tower with terrace and the large crenellated portal, complete with a wall walk, push the viewer's gaze skywards, arousing their imagination. In the internal courtyard, whose sober architectural fabric is harmoniously balanced, one almost feels spied upon

querce
SAFFO
EUGENIO MONTALE

by the time-worn statues that peer out from the parapets. The main facade in the courtyard is elegantly marked by an outdoor staircase leading to the top floor and by four pilaster strips that end with the arches of the loggia in the corridor. At the center of the courtyard, a column crowned by a cross confirms the religious identity of this family of remote Catholic origins, while to the right a huge bougainvillea clambers up the second tower, which only resembles a tower and is instead an architectural sleight of hand. On the ground floor, a door leads to the service rooms, which at one time hosted a large room with silkworms, the weaving with traditional looms, and a laboratory, and today hosts an old kitchen with a rustic air. On the wall, an ancient map proudly shows the position of the small and mostly unknown Depressa. Above, a long corridor featuring large windows and a star-shaped vault marks the alternating of the rooms. The sunlight of Italy's Mezzogiorno filters in through the openings and further emphasizes the floor made of cement tiles featuring two-tone lozenges. The rooms are stuck in the past, no concession made to modernization except to that which is necessary, seeing that at one time the castle had only one bathroom. The interior furnishings, which are almost entirely from the nineteenth century, speak of a countryside nobility that has never cared about showing off and that simply wanted to recount the past via everyday life. Sitting rooms, bedrooms, simplicity is the rule here. Vanity is banned. Everything reminds us of the aplomb of a grandiose and beautiful lady, in spite of the wrinkles that have started to furrow her face. Even if time has left its mark, dignity and elegance remain unchanged. Hanging on the walls are many family portraits, gorgeous women in gowns worn for important soirées or knitting, like Countess Albina Guicciardi of Cervarolo, an ancestor of Edoardo and Francesco. And then there are books whose leather bindings have been consumed by time, a huge collection of crockery from all around Europe, banners, medals, and certificates, like a museum of memory speaking of the family's many public and political achievements. Added to this are the Winspeare family's coats of arms, and two paintings portraying Naples, a memory of the family's first Italian home.

The rear facade follows the same rationale as the main facade in a much more austere way, but with a variation: a large terrace covered by vaults overlooking the garden that offers the visitor a lovely stroll, with sheltered corners, intimate "alcoves" with benches, sofas, and white-painted stone tables. The natural landscape, dotted with lavender and rosemary plants, is the perfect place to grow vines, roses, and jasmines. There is also a lemon, orange, and tangerine grove, all enriching the air with their fragrance. The spontaneous almond trees are mixed with the false peppers characterized by twisting and evocative trunks, alongside privets, a large agave, centuries-old maritime pines, wisteria, and fruit trees. Up close to the castle, a maze of Chinese bamboo with leaves the shape of swallows' tails fades into an undergrowth of periwinkles, adding a touch of mystery and wonder. As one walks along the path, the sound of one's footsteps merges with the rustling of the leaves swaying in the summer wind. The sunlight filters in between the tall reeds, creating a play of shadow and light dancing on the ground. The air is permeated by the fragrance of the aromatic herbs and the citrus plants, an inebriating mixture. The north wind brings with it the sound of nature: the singing of the birds, the chirruping of the cicadas, the whispering of the leaves. In a never-ending whorl of past lives, in the delicate balance of an instant of beauty.

9.

Family memories, comprised of prints, paintings, drawings, sculptures, and photographs.

To the right, the living room decorated with medals and certificates that tell of the Winspeares' public and political accomplishments, along with the coats of arms of the family and two paintings from Naples, a memento of their first Italian home.

AVVISO

*One of the living rooms, adorned with armchairs,
ottomans, and original period furnishings.
To the left, time seems to have stopped in this dining room,
whose walls are furnished with two large display cases filled to the hilt with a collection
of dishes from all around Europe.*

Front cover
The entrance courtyard to the home
of Francesca Marciano in Spongano.

Back cover
The dining area, opening onto the garden,
of La Casa dei Disegni (The House of Drawings) in Spongano.

All photographs are by
Filippo Bamberghi

Drawings
Gianni Veneziano

Editorial Project Manager
Valentina Lindon

Art Direction and Graphic Design
Cristina Menotti

Translation
Sylvia Adrian Notini

Distributed in English throughout the World by
Rizzoli International Publications, Inc.
49 West 27th Street
New York, NY 10001
www.rizzoliusa.com

ISBN: 978-88-918431-3-5

Printed in Italy
2025 2026 2027 2028 / 10 9 8 7 6 5 4 3 2 1

The authorized representative in the EU for safety
and compliance is Mondadori Libri S.p.A.,
via Gian Battista Vico 42, Milan, Italy, 20123,
http://www.mondadori.it

Visit us online:
Instagram.com/RizzoliBooks
Facebook.com/RizzoliNewYork
X: @Rizzoli_Books
Youtube.com/user/RizzoliNY

*Heartfelt thanks go to my friends
and to all the kind souls who
believed in me and in this
"dream," generously sharing
their passions and knowledge
so it could become a reality.
The names to remember are many,
and I want to express
my gratitude to every one of them
for what they gave me.
I wish to thank Gianni, my
partner in life and work, whose
creativity continues to inspire
and guide me along our path
together, and Virginia, my
talented daughter, whom I hope
will have endless happiness
and a sense of curiosity, so that
she can always explore the world
through eyes filled with wonder.
Special thanks go to Patrizia
Piccinini for having chosen words
that give a shape to all this
beauty, and to Filippo Bamberghi,
who was able to eternalize
moments of infinity through
the magic of photography.*
L.D.V.

A·D·